Gita for Young Minds

Sunita Pant Bansal is a renowned mythologist, storyteller, and author with a career that spans over four decades. Throughout her journey, she has worn many hats, excelling as a writer, editor, publisher, and entrepreneur.

She has headed publishing houses and founded and edited newspapers and magazines for readers in India, US and UK. Her contributions to the world of literature extend across multiple platforms, working with prestigious organizations such as Walt Disney, Warner Bros., Pearson Education, The Times of India, Hindustan Times, and ABP Group.

In addition to her global collaborations, Sunita ran her own publishing house creating books for audiences worldwide and served as the President of the esteemed Institute of Indology, further cementing her influence in the literary world.

Sunita has authored innumerable children's books focused on folk literature and scriptures, which have been translated into multiple languages and sold across the globe. She has also written over 30 books for adults and young readers, delving into the philosophy of mythology. Her books explore and reinterpret the timeless tales of characters from the epics and foundational texts for modern readers. Her storytelling blends mythology with history, making ancient tales accessible in today's context.

Sunita's contributions to publishing and literature have earned her recognition, including the 2024 AALEKH Women Achievers Award.

Amongst Sunita's recent bestsellers are *Krishna: The Management Guru, Everyday Gita, Puranas: The Origin of Gods and Goddesses, Ramayan: The Journey of Ram, Mahabharat: The Rise and fall of Heroes.*

Website: www.sunitapantbansal.com
Social media:
LinkedIn & Instagram: @sunitapantbansal
Twitter & Facebook: @sunitapb

Other books published by Rupa Publications:

Krishna The Management Guru

Everyday Gita

The Illusion of Illusions: Yashodhara's Story

Gita

for Young Minds

Sunita Pant Bansal

MOONSTONE

Published in Moonstone
by Rupa Publications India Pvt. Ltd 2025
7/16, Ansari Road, Daryaganj
New Delhi 110002

Sales centres:
Bengaluru Chennai
Hyderabad Jaipur Kathmandu
Kolkata Mumbai Prayagraj

P-ISBN: 978-93-6156-606-6
E-ISBN: 978-93-6156-731-5

First impression 2025

10 9 8 7 6 5 4 3 2 1

Printed in India

Dedicated to Ija, my paternal grandmother,
who sowed the seeds of storytelling in me by her own
inimitable style of retelling mythology.

Contents

Preface *ix*

The CONTEXT *xiii*

1. ARJUN'S DILEMMA sets the stage 1
2. Krishna imparts DIVINE KNOWLEDGE 10
3. Krishna explains KARMA YOGA 20
4. Krishna explains GYAN YOGA 31
5. Krishna explains RENUNCIATION 41
6. Krishna explains DHYAN YOGA 49
7. Krishna explains ULTIMATE WISDOM 60
8. Krishna explains the ETERNAL SPIRIT 69
9. Krishna reveals the DIVINE MYSTERY 77
10. Krishna explains his MANIFESTATIONS 88
11. Krishna reveals his own COSMIC FORM 97
12. Krishna explains BHAKTI YOGA 106
13. Krishna explains CREATION AND CREATOR 114
14. Krishna explains the THREE MODES OF NATURE 124
15. Krishna explains the SUPREME PERSON 134

Preface

The development of our body and our senses, in childhood, is governed by the soul. We grow naturally, organically. But as we grow older, we become aware of this growth, and our senses. Our desires get roused by the temptations around us, helped by the genetic tendencies that we carry within us. These desires start to gain control of our body. Our mind's discriminatory power is pushed aside. Self-control is lost. Once bad habits are firmly established, the wisdom gets lost, or we can say that it hides within the deep recesses of our mind.

When desires or bad habits are in control of our body, they do not want to let it go easily. So, a battle must be fought inside ourselves to get back our self-control, for which we need to dig out our wisdom from hiding. This is the battle of Mahabharata.

In the larger picture, we see wars being fought between nations; people quarrelling amongst themselves. There are fights within families, siblings and among friends. The main reason for any quarrel or disagreement is that people are not able to let go of their selfish motives and desires. All problems can be solved peacefully if people see both sides of the issue and work out an agreement. We all know that yet...wars continue being fought for possession and power. And this has been going on since forever.

In the story of Mahabharata, Krishna urges Arjun to fight for his rights. It was his duty as a warrior to fight a declared war (declared by his own cousin Duryodhan) and establish peace, law and order in the kingdom. At the same time, Krishna also advises him not to kill needlessly; saving lives is always more important.

All of us face dilemmas or are confused at some or the other point in our lives, as was Arjun when he realized that his so-called enemies were his own family and friends. Krishna told him that it was normal to be confused, but in such a situation we should keep faith in the righteous action. And then he goes on to explain about righteous actions.

Any act that may cause others harm would be considered as sin. But, at times life puts us in a position where any action we do would be causing harm to someone or the other. For instance, in a situation of a robber entering a village to rob and kill people, it would be more sensible to kill one robber to save lives of many villagers.

Right in the middle of the battlefield of Kurukshetra, in his sermon called the Bhagavad Gita (Gita in short), Krishna teaches Arjun, how to face such confusing situations in life.

First of all, there is no shame in accepting that you don't know what the right thing to do is. In fact, it is the first step to finding the answer. That is exactly what Arjun did. He decided to resolve his confusion right there and then. How? He turned to Krishna for advice.

Since all that advice is contained in Gita, the book serves like a helpline for when we feel cornered in life. In the fast pace of life that we lead today, feeling cornered or confused or stressed is not limited to adults anymore. Sadly, children are also going through the same gamut of emotions.

Allegorically speaking, our mind is blind like King Dhritarashtra, giving birth to impulsive mental tendencies, the Kauravas. Our intellect is like Pandu, who gives birth to self-disciplinary tendencies, the Pandavas. Our life is the battlefield of Kurukshetra, where we face the battle between our emotional impulses and self-disciplinary thoughts every day. It is the same for children as for adults.

Since emotional impulses always outnumber the self-disciplinary thoughts, we need to seek help from our hidden wisdom. But it is hidden really deep. How do we find it? Through Gita of course! As Arjun was guided by Krishna's Gita to discover his own wisdom, so shall we be.

Gita for Young Minds is specially simplified to make it easy for them to understand and imbibe its wisdom. Each chapter starts with its gist and a selection of important *shlokas* with their meanings, followed by an extremely relatable story-like explanation. The chapter ends with a popular fable illustrating the essence of what Krishna is telling Arjun.

The purpose of the book is to introduce the timeless practical wisdom of Gita at the very foundational level of a person. As a strong foundation is crucial to any building's life, so is the case with our lives.

Sunita Pant Bansal

The CONTEXT

Hastinapur was a prosperous kingdom in the north of India, ruled by the renowned Kuru dynasty. But later this dynasty was ripped apart by conflict that led to a big battle on the plains of Kurukshetra.

King Shantanu of Hastinapur had a son named Devavrata, also known as Bhishma, who had taken a vow to never marry. Shantanu's two other sons had died early. Sage Vyasa had then blessed the Kuru family with three sons, Dhritarashtra, Vidur and Pandu. Dhritarashtra was born blind and Vidur was born to a maid of the palace. So, it was Pandu who became the king.

However, due to a twist of fate, Pandu had to go away to the Himalayan forests with his wives Kunti and Madri. There, five sons were born to him through the blessings of gods Dharma, Pavan, Indra and the Ashwinikumars. Three of them, Yudhishthir, Bheem and Arjun were born to Kunti. And Nakul and Sahadev were born to Madri. These five sons of Pandu were called Pandavas.

Back in the palace, Dhritarashtra became the king of Hastinapur. He and his wife Gandhari had a hundred sons, called Kauravas, and one daughter. The eldest two sons were Duryodhan and Duhshasan.

Pandu and Madri died in the forest. Kunti returned to the palace with the Pandavas. All the princes—the hundred Kauravas and the five Pandavas—were given rigorous training in archery, wrestling, mace-fight and other skills of warfare.

Everyone considered Yudhishthir to be the natural heir to the throne of Hastinapur, but Duryodhan hated his cousins, the Pandavas. He felt, that being the reigning king's son, he was the rightful heir. Shakuni, Duryodhan's maternal uncle, fanned his hatred for the Pandavas. And blind Dhritarashtra was so fond of his son that he never corrected him.

Duryodhan once tried to poison and drown Bheem, the strongest of the Pandavas, but was unsuccessful. Finally, with Shakuni's help, he plotted to burn all five brothers alive in a house made of lac.

The resourceful Pandavas were able to save themselves, but let the world believe that they were dead. Disguised as *brahmins*, they moved from place to place.

In the kingdom of Panchal, at an archery competition arranged by King Drupad, Arjun won the hand of his daughter Draupadi, also called Panchali. On Kunti's advice, Draupadi became wife to all five Pandavas.

Krishna, who was Kunti's nephew, was also there at the archery competition. He recognized the Pandavas in spite of their disguise.

Realizing that the Pandavas were not dead, Dhritarashtra called them back and gave them a forested area, called Khandavaprastha, as their share of the family property.

The Pandavas settled down there with their new bride Draupadi and began to develop the place. The Pandavas built their capital at Khandavaprastha, which eventually came to be known as Indraprastha.

Duryodhan grew envious of Yudhishthir's increasing power and prestige. His uncle Shakuni came up with another evil plan. Yudhishthir was

challenged to a game of dice at Hastinapur and was tricked out of all his possessions–his kingdom, wealth, brothers and even his wife. Eventually Dhritarashtra set the Pandavas free to go back to Indraprastha.

But on Shakuni's advice, Duryodhan again invited Yudhishthir to a game of dice. This time the condition was that if Yudhishthir lost, he would hand over his kingdom to Duryodhan for twelve years and retire to the forest with his brothers and Draupadi. At the end of those twelve years, all of them would have to live somewhere in disguise. If they were caught before the year was out, they would have to serve the term all over again.

This time too, Yudhishthir lost to Shakuni's trickery. With Draupadi and his brothers, he had to leave for the forest. At the end of twelve years, the Pandavas hid themselves in Viratnagar, the capital of the kingdom of Matsya, as employees of King Virat.

It so happened that a neighbouring king attacked the kingdom of Viratnagar. King Virat set out with his soldiers, accompanied by his new employees Yudhishthir, Bheem, Nakul and Sahadev. Just then Kauravas came to Viratnagar and began to take away all the cattle. It was Arjun, in his disguise as a dance-master, who rushed to save the cattle.

By now, one year of living in hiding for Pandavas was over. They revealed their identity to King Virat. Duryodhan jumped at this opportunity and declared that by fighting in a way only Arjun could have, he had given himself away before the year of hiding was fully over. According to him, by the terms and conditions of the second game of dice, the Pandavas were now due for another round of exile and hiding. As could be seen, Duryodhan was not interested in sharing his kingdom with his cousins.

There were negotiations for peace, led by Krishna himself, but Duryodhan refused to yield. Finally, Kauravas and Pandavas came to battle on the plains of Kurukshetra.

1

ARJUN'S DILEMMA sets the stage

On the battlefield of Kurukshetra, on the first day of the battle, Arjun asks his charioteer friend, Krishna, to drive his chariot between the two armies. Seeing his friends and relatives on the opposite side as his enemies, whom he must kill to win the war, Arjun feels a tremendous wave of compassion overcoming him. He does not want to kill his own kith and kin, hence refuses to fight.

Dhritarashtra uvācha
dharma-kṣhetre kuru-kṣhetre samavetā yuyutsavaḥ
māmakāḥ pāṇḍavāśhchaiva kimakurvata Sanjaya (1.1)

Dhritarashtra asks: O Sanjay, after gathering on the holy field of Kurukshetra, and desiring to fight, what are my sons and the sons of Pandu doing? (1.1)

Sanjay uvācha
dṛiṣhṭvā tu pāṇḍavānīkaṁ vyūḍhaṁ duryodhanastadā
āchāryamupasaṅgamya rājā vachanamabravīt (1.2)

Sanjay says: On observing the Pandava army standing in military formation, King Duryodhan has approached his teacher Dronacharya to talk. (1.2)

Duryodhan uvācha
aparyāptaṁ tadasmākaṁ balaṁ bhīṣhmābhirakṣhitam
paryāptaṁ tvidameteṣhāṁ balaṁ bhīmābhirakṣhitam (1.10)
ayaneṣhu cha sarveṣhu yathā-bhāgamavasthitāḥ
bhīṣhmamevābhirakṣhantu bhavantaḥ sarva eva hi (1.11)

Duryodhan says: Our army defended by Bhishma is insufficient but the army of theirs defended by Bheem is sufficient. Therefore, I call upon all the generals of the Kaurava army now to give full support to Grandsire Bhishma, even as you defend your respective strategic points. (1.10-11)

Arjun uvācha
senayor ubhayor madhye rathaṁ sthāpaya me 'chyuta (1.21)
yāvadetān nirīkṣhe 'haṁ yoddhu-kāmān avasthitān
kairmayā saha yoddhavyam asmin raṇa-samudyame (1.22)

na kāṅkṣhe vijayaṁ Krishna na cha rājyaṁ sukhāni cha
kiṁ no rājyena govinda kiṁ bhogair jīvitena vā (1.32)
yeṣhām arthe kāṅkṣhitaṁ no rājyaṁ bhogāḥ sukhāni cha
ta ime 'vasthitā yuddhe prāṇāṁs tyaktvā dhanāni cha (1.33)

yady apy ete na paśhyanti lobhopahata-chetasaḥ
kula-kṣhaya-kṛitaṁ doṣhaṁ mitra-drohe cha pātakam (1.38)

kathaṁ na jñeyam asmābhiḥ pāpād asmān nivartitum
kula-kṣhaya-kṛitaṁ doṣhaṁ prapaśhyadbhir Janardan (1.39)

Arjun says: O Krishna, place my chariot in between both the armies so that I may survey those who stand here eager to fight. Let me know on the eve of this battle with whom I have to fight. (1.21-22)

I do not desire victory, kingdom, or the happiness resulting from it. Of what use will be a kingdom, pleasures, or even life itself, when the very persons for whom we want them, are standing before us for battle? (1.32-33)

Their thoughts are overpowered by greed, and they see no wrong in annihilating their relatives or wreaking treachery upon friends. Yet, O Janardan, why should we, who can clearly see the crime in killing our kith and kin, not turn away from this sin? (1.38-39)

Sanjay uvācha
evam uktvārjunaḥ saṅkhye rathopastha upāviśhat
visṛijya sa-śharaṁ chāpaṁ śhoka-saṁvigna-mānasaḥ (1.47)

Sanjay says: Speaking thus, Arjun cast aside his bow and arrows, and sank into the seat of his chariot, his mind in distress and overwhelmed with grief. (1.47)

A mighty war was set to begin on the battlefield of Kurukshetra. The Pandava and Kaurava armies had assembled.

On one side of the battlefield stood giant battalions

comprising chariots, elephants, horsemen and foot soldiers, headed by their commander Bhishma, the grand-uncle of Pandavas and Kauravas. This was the Kaurava army.

On the other side of the field was a smaller army, headed by commander Drishtadyumna, Draupadi's brother. Though lesser in number, the Pandava army radiated hope and confidence. After all, they were fighting for justice!

Far away in the capital city of Hastinapur, King Dhritarashtra sat on the royal throne, wondering aloud about the great war that was due to commence any moment between his sons and the sons of his brother. His head told him that his hundred mighty sons were backed by powerful regional kings and Krishna's own army, the *Narayani Sena*, so the Kauravas should definitely win. But the blind king's heart knew that the Pandavas had truth and Krishna on their side, so how could they lose!

Dhritarashtra turned to his advisor, the clairvoyant Sanjay, and asked, "What is happening on the holy field of Kurukshetra where my sons and sons of my brother Pandu have gathered to fight?"

In the entire Gita, this was the only time the king spoke, the rest of the verses are Sanjay's report about the goings-on on the battlefield, something like a news reporter's eyewitness account of the event.

How did Sanjay do that without being present on the site of the war?

He was blessed by sage Vyasa with divine vision

and hearing, which enabled him to see and hear the events unfolding on the battlefield of Kurukshetra.

Sanjay focussed his attention on to the battlefield and started reporting...

Duryodhan seems worried on seeing the extraordinary confidence of the Pandava army. He heads towards his guru, Drona. Emphasizing the names of the great Pandava warriors, he reminds Drona of Drishtadyumna's vow of eliminating him. As if this provocation was not enough, Duryodhan expresses his doubts about their own commander-in-chief. He knew Bhishma's heart was soft towards his other grand nephews, the Pandavas.

"There are many heroic warriors fighting with Arjun and Bheem no doubt, but we also have a fair share of powerful fighters with us, like you, Guruji, your son Ashwatthama, Kripa, Karna and the invincible Bhishma Pitamah. If all our commanders make sure that he is kept safe, we should do well in the war."

Drona does not respond to Duryodhan's provocative comments, but Bhishma does by standing in his golden chariot and roaring like a lion. He then blows his conch loudly, announcing that the Kauravas were ready to fight till death.

Immediately, from the far side of the field, another golden chariot, flying the flag of Hanuman, comes forward. Two conches sound in unison—Krishna's Panchajanya and Arjun's Devadatta. Behind them, the other Pandava brothers, Bheem, Yudhishthir, Nakul and Sahadev also blow their respective conches.

All around there is an uproar of soldiers shouting, horses neighing and elephants trumpeting.

Arjun wants to see what he is up against before commencing the war. So Krishna, his dear friend and charioteer, brings their chariot to the front line for an overview.

Seeing his esteemed teachers, Guru Dronacharya, Guru Kripacharya, his beloved uncles, cousins, nephews, grandnephews, fathers-in-law, brothers-in-law and his granduncle, on the other side, Arjun is overwhelmed with grief. The enormity of what he is about to do strikes him like a thunderbolt. His knees buckle, his hands shake and his bow, the magnificent Gandiva, slips from his grasp.

"How can I fight my near and dear ones, Krishna!" Arjun exclaims. "I cannot fight this battle. I do not wish any wealth or kingdom. What use is victory if my loved ones are not there for me?"

Arjun refuses to fight even though he knew that the Kauravas had wronged his family.

"O Krishna, war brings only misery and disaster. I cannot kill my loved ones. Let them kill me instead!" So saying, he drops his bow and sinks down in despair.

It was then that Krishna comes forward and teaches Arjun how the righteous path was not always an easy one. One had to be willing to fight for what one believed to be right, even if it meant sacrificing one's own life.

This sermon of 700 verses came to be known as the Bhagavad Gita.

There's a story in Mahabharata that helps to understand Arjun's dilemma...

One evening, a merchant was returning home after selling his wares. Unknown to him, a robber had been stalking him for a while. Suddenly, while walking along a deserted path, on the edge of a forest, the merchant realized that he was being followed. Since he was carrying a lot of money, he panicked and started running. He didn't want to be robbed. The robber, who had every intention of robbing the merchant, also ran after him.

The merchant quickly entered the forest, hoping to dodge the robber. As he was trying to find a place to hide, he came across a hermit meditating under a tree. Paying his respects to the old hermit, as was the norm of those times, the merchant went on further to hide. It was getting dark, and the forest looked scary, but the merchant had to save himself from the robber.

Meanwhile, the robber also managed to reach the hermit. Without wasting any time, he asked the old man if he had seen anyone pass by.

It was clear to the hermit that the scared-looking merchant was running away from this harsh-looking robber. Now hermits, as a rule, are harmless people. They live a simple, solitary life in the forests, meditating. They eat whatever they are able to find in the forest, which would normally be fruits and roots. They never steal, nor do they tell lies. They are not scared of wild animals and the animals are also not scared of them.

So, when the robber asked about the merchant, the hermit told him the truth. Pleased with the information, the robber went in the direction pointed out by the old man and soon found the merchant. The poor merchant was robbed and killed.

All of us face similar situations in our lives, where our decisions—through following our principles—may cause harm to others. It is important to evaluate the situation in the context of larger good before reaching a decision. For instance, the hermit could have avoided telling the truth and saved the merchant. His truth killed the man that his lie could have saved.

Arjun was in a similar dilemma. He did not want to hurt or kill his relatives. Krishna explained to him that when two noble principles are in conflict, it is important to see which of them is higher. Saving a life is a higher principle than telling the truth.

But sometimes, a few lives may have to be taken to protect more lives, like when an army kills the enemy to protect their motherland.

It is okay to be confused or conflicted. And in such a situation, the sensible course of action would be to do what Arjun did–seek help.

2

Krishna imparts DIVINE KNOWLEDGE

Krishna imparts divine knowledge to Arjun. He explains the immortal nature of the soul and the difference between body and soul. Krishna reminds Arjun of his responsibility as a warrior, and that he should do his duty to the best of his ability without worrying about success or failure. To do this efficiently, Arjun would need to control his sensory desires.

Shri Bhagavan uvācha
klaibyaṁ mā sma gamaḥ Parth naitat tvayyupapadyate
kṣhudraṁ hṛidaya-daurbalyaṁ tyaktvottiṣhṭha parantapa
(2.03)

Krishna said: Do not become a coward, O Arjun, because it does not befit you. Shake off this trivial weakness of your heart and get up for the battle, O conqueror of enemies. (2.03)

Arjun uvācha
kathaṁ bhīṣhmam ahaṁ sankhye droṇaṁ cha Madhusudan
iṣhubhiḥ pratiyotsyāmi pūjārhāvari-sūdana (2.04)

Arjun said: How can I strike my grandfather, my guru, and all other relatives, who are worthy of my respect, with arrows in battle, O Krishna? (2.04)

Shrī Bhagavan uvācha
aśhochyān-anvaśhochas-tvaṁ prajñā-vādānśh cha bhāṣhase
gatāsūn-agatāsūnśh-cha nānuśhochanti paṇḍitāḥ (2.11)

Krishna said: You grieve for those who are not worthy of grief, and yet speak words of wisdom. The wise grieve neither for the living nor for the dead. (2.11)

na tvevāhaṁ jātu nāsaṁ na tvaṁ neme janādhipāḥ
na chaiva na bhaviṣhyāmaḥ sarve vayamataḥ param (2.12)

There was never a time when these monarchs, you or I did not exist; nor shall we ever cease to exist in the future. (2.12)

nāsato vidyate bhāvo nābhāvo vidyate sataḥ
ubhayorapi dṛiṣhṭo 'nta stvanayos tattva-darśhibhiḥ (2.16)

The invisible soul is eternal, and the visible physical body is transitory. The reality of these two is indeed known to men of wisdom. (2.16)

na jāyate mriyate vā kadāchin nāyaṁ bhūtvā bhavitā vā na bhūyaḥ
ajo nityaḥ śhāśhvato 'yaṁ purāṇo na hanyate hanyamāne śharīre (2.20)

The soul is neither born nor does it die at any time. It does not come into being nor cease to exist. It is unborn, eternal, immortal, and ageless. The soul is not destroyed when the body is destroyed. (2.20)

vāsānsi jīrṇāni yathā vihāya navāni gṛihṇāti naro 'parāṇi
tathā śharīrāṇi vihāya jīrṇānya nyāni sanyāti navāni dehī
(2.22)

As a person sheds worn-out garments and wears new ones, likewise, at the time of death, the soul casts off its worn-out body and enters a new one. (2.22)

nainaṁ chhindanti śhastrāṇi nainaṁ dahati pāvakaḥ
na chainaṁ kledayantyāpo na śhoṣhayati mārutaḥ (2.23)
achchhedyo 'yam adāhyo 'yam akledyo 'śhoṣhya eva cha
nityaḥ sarva-gataḥ sthāṇur achalo 'yaṁ sanātanaḥ (2.24)

Weapons do not cut the soul, fire does not burn it, water does not make it wet, and the wind does not make it dry. The soul is eternal, all pervading, unchanging, immovable, and primal. (2.23-24)

atha chainaṁ nitya-jātaṁ nityaṁ vā manyase mṛitam
tathāpi tvaṁ mahā-bāho naivaṁ śhochitum arhasi (2.26)
jātasya hi dhruvo mṛityur dhruvaṁ janma mṛitasya cha
tasmād aparihārye 'rthe na tvaṁ śhochitum arhasi (2.27)

If you think that the physical body takes birth and dies perpetually, even then, you should not grieve. Because death is certain for the one who is born, and birth is certain for the one who dies. Therefore, you should not lament over the inevitable. (2.26-27)

karmaṇy-evādhikāras te mā phaleṣhu kadāchana
mā karma-phala-hetur bhūr mā te saṅgo 'stvakarmaṇi
(2.47)

You have control over doing your respective duty only, but no control or claim over the results. The fruits of work should not be your motive, and you should never be inactive. (2.47)

prajahāti yadā kāmān sarvān Parth mano-gatān
ātmany-evātmanā tuṣhṭaḥ sthita-prajñas tadochyate (2.55)

When one is completely free from all desires of the mind and is satisfied and happy with the universal Spirit, then one is called an enlightened person. (2.55)

dhyāyato viṣhayān puṁsaḥ saṅgas teṣhūpajāyate
saṅgāt sañjāyate kāmaḥ kāmāt krodho 'bhijāyate (2.62)

While contemplating on the objects of senses, one develops attachment to them. Attachment leads to desire, and from desire arises anger. (2.62)

indriyāṇāṁ hi charatāṁ yan mano 'nuvidhīyate
tadasya harati prajñāṁ vāyur nāvam ivāmbhasi (2.67)

Just as a strong wind sweeps a boat off its chartered course on the water, any one of the senses on which the mind focuses can lead the intellect astray. (2,67)

eṣhā brāhmī sthitiḥ Parth naināṁ prāpya vimuhyati
sthitvāsyām anta-kāle 'pi brahma-nirvāṇam ṛichchhati
(2.72)

O Parth, such is the state of an enlightened soul, that having attained it, one is no longer deluded. Being established in this state, even at the hour of death, one is liberated from the cycle of life and death and becomes one with God. (2.72)

Initially, Krishna tried to provoke a very desolate looking Arjun, "Get up Arjun. Let not this dilemma rule over your mind. Do not behave like a coward!"

Arjun was not provoked. Rather, he seemed to have sunk further in despair.

Krishna continued, "You know very well that your enemies are not thinking about your well-being. To oppress others is a sin but to tolerate oppression is a far greater sin. This war is no ordinary war, it is *Dharmayuddha*—the battle of righteousness. It is a battle between right and wrong."

"How can killing my cousins and teachers be right!" retorted Arjun instantly.

"All those whom you claim to be your relatives, are none but individual unrelated souls. They always did and always will exist, though in different forms. It's the same for you and me," Krishna tried to explain.

Arjun looked far from convinced. The only thing he knew and understood well was that when he shot an arrow at someone, that person was sure to die!

"What is it that really dies when a person dies? Only their physical body." Krishna seemed to read Arjun's troubled mind.

"But their souls, their true essence, the invisible spirit, cannot be destroyed, ever. The soul is indestructible. It is never born, and it never dies. Even if you kill anyone, their souls will remain alive. So do not worry Kunti-putra, just pick up your bow and fight. This is your duty as a warrior."

Krishna then explained the fundamental distinction between temporary material body and eternal spiritual soul.

"No weapon can cut the soul, no fire can burn it. Water cannot drench it, nor can the wind dry it. Death is simply a change of body for the soul, like a change of clothes. We, the eternal spiritual soul, have no reason for having grief over death of the temporary body. The elements that form the body return to nature after death and again form another body, another life."

"Soul is indestructible, immeasurable, unborn and eternal. Childhood, youth, old age and death are attributed to the body and not to the soul. The sensory feelings of pain and pleasure are transitory. We should ignore them."

Arjun was not satisfied with Krishna's explanation. He knew that war always resulted in deaths. In this case, he was likely to lose his family members, ones he had grown up with and played with.

Krishna understood his friend's pain, but continued, "Those who are wise, cry neither for living nor for dead. Everything exists eternally. Although there is always some pain in losing our loved ones, the wise undergo that pain with patience and tolerance. They carry on without letting grief overwhelm their lives and disrupt their responsibilities."

"Carry on? I feel like renouncing everything and retiring to the forest in peace instead! Krishna my friend, please show me the way through this dark hour of my life," Arjun pleaded.

"Renounce everything!" Krishna exclaimed. "Do not ever think that you will be praised for your renunciation. In fact, you will be blamed for centuries to come for running away from the battlefield. Every generation will make fun of your cowardice, Arjun!"

"You must understand that our *dharma* lies in performing our duty sincerely to the best of our ability. You are a *kshatriya*. Your *dharma* is to maintain order, to defend what is good and just, by force if necessary. Fighting this *Dharmayuddha* is the need of the hour. So, stand up and fight this battle! Do not think of the consequences, as they are not in your control, only the action is."

Arjun wondered how to avoid thinking about the consequences. It was not easy.

Seeing his friend lost in thoughts, Krishna added further, "Know the truth Arjun—whoever is born has to die and whoever is dead has to be reborn. A man who has no knowledge, thinks that he is a body with a soul, but in reality, he is a soul with a body. Lack of this knowledge is the cause of grief. So, know yourself O Parth, and be free forever."

Krishna then went on to explain the real meaning of freedom.

"We are constantly controlled by our senses, creating desires in us for sense objects, eventually resulting in our forming attachments to those objects. If we do not get—or worse still—lose what we desire, it makes us angry, unhappy or confused. And we might end up doing something wrong, or hurtful."

Arjun could relate to this and slowly began to understand his own dilemma.

Pleased with his friend's progress, Krishna continued, "The trick is to focus only on our action without thinking about the consequences. Like a tortoise who withdraws its limbs into its shell and becomes still, so does a wise person withdraw his senses into himself and remains calm. Such a person is free from all desires, hence no attachments. Having such steady wisdom is the real freedom."

Focus was never a problem with Arjun, as he had shown many times in archery. According to a popular story, after Pandu's death, the Pandavas and Kauravas lived together in Hastinapur and studied martial arts and warfare under Guru Drona.

Once Drona decided to test the young boys. He placed a wooden bird in a tall tree and asked the boys to slice off its head with a single arrow. The young Pandavas and Kauravas were excited and raring to show their archery skills. But no, there was yet another preliminary test before the final shooting!

Drona called the young boys one by one and made them stand at the spot from where they were supposed to shoot at the bird. Then he asked them what all they could see. All of them came up with descriptions of the tree, its branches, leaves, the colour of the wooden bird and even the sky. Except one young boy—Arjun. He was very clear that he could only see the bird's head and nothing more.

The answer pleased Drona, as it showed Arjun to be absolutely focussed on his target. The rest of the boys were distracted by the background. It goes without saying that Arjun shot the arrow and successfully sliced off the bird's head.

Krishna wanted Arjun to apply the same focus to fighting the war, and not be distracted by who was fighting who.

3

Krishna explains KARMA YOGA

Krishna talks about two paths—of knowledge and action—to peace and happiness in life. The path chosen depends on individuals, whether they are thinkers or doers. It is easy for most people to follow the path of Karma Yoga, the path of action, which entails doing our duty to the best of our ability. Krishna advises to think about the results of an action before taking it up. He also says that desires must be controlled, as unfulfilled desires give rise to anger pushing us towards sinful actions.

Arjun uvācha
jyāyasī chet karmaṇas te matā buddhir Janardan
tat kiṁ karmaṇi ghore māṁ niyojayasi keśhava (3.01)
vyāmiśhreṇeva vākyena buddhiṁ mohayasīva me
tad ekaṁ vada niśhchitya yena śhreyo 'ham āpnuyām (3.02)

Arjun asked: If you consider that acquiring steady wisdom is better than working, then why do you want me to engage in this horrible war, O Krishna? You seem to confuse my mind by apparently conflicting words. Tell me, decisively, one thing by which I may attain the Supreme. (3.01-02)

Shrī Bhagavan uvācha
loke 'smin dvi-vidhā niṣhṭhā purā proktā mayānagha
jñāna-yogena sāṅkhyānāṁ karma-yogena yoginām (3.03)

Krishna said: In this world there is a twofold path of spiritual discipline. The path of self-knowledge for the contemplative ones, and the path of selfless work for all the others. (3.03)

na karmaṇām anārambhān naiṣhkarmyaṁ puruṣho 'śhnute
na cha sannyasanād eva siddhiṁ samadhigachchhati (3.04)
na hi kaśhchit kṣhaṇam api jātu tiṣhṭhatyakarma-kṛit
kāryate hyavaśhaḥ karma sarvaḥ prakṛiti-jair guṇaiḥ (3.05)

One does not attain freedom from the bondage of Karma by merely abstaining from work. No one attains perfection by merely giving up work, because no one can remain actionless even for a moment. Everyone is driven to action by the forces of Nature. (3.04-05)

niyataṁ kuru karma tvaṁ karma jyāyo hyakarmaṇaḥ
śharīra-yātrāpi cha te na prasiddhyed akarmaṇaḥ (3.08)

Perform your obligatory duty, because working is indeed better than sitting idle. Even the maintenance of your body would not be possible without work. (3.08)

saha-yajñāḥ prajāḥ sṛiṣhṭvā purovācha prajāpatiḥ
anena prasaviṣhyadhvam eṣha vo 'stviṣhṭa-kāma-dhuk
(3.10)

In the beginning the creator created human beings along with selfless service (yagya) and said—by serving each other you shall prosper, and the selfless service shall fulfil all your desires. (3.10)

devān bhāvayatānena te devā bhāvayantu vaḥ
parasparaṁ bhāvayantaḥ śhreyaḥ param avāpsyatha (3.11)

Nourish the celestial controllers with selfless service, and they will nourish you. Thus nourishing one another you shall attain the Supreme goal. (3.11)

iṣhṭān bhogān hi vo devā dāsyante yajña-bhāvitāḥ
tair dattān apradāyaibhyo yo bhuṅkte stena eva saḥ (3.12)

The celestial controllers, served by selfless service, will give you all desired objects. One who enjoys the gift of celestial controllers without sharing with others is a thief indeed. (3.12)

yajña-śhiṣhṭāśhinaḥ santo muchyante sarva-kilbiṣhaiḥ
bhuñjate te tvaghaṁ pāpā ye pachantyātma-kāraṇāt (3.13)

The righteous ones who eat after feeding others are freed from all sins. But the impious ones who cook food only for themselves, without first offering to God, or sharing with others, actually eat sin. (3.13)

karmaṇaiva hi sansiddhim āsthitā janakādayaḥ
loka-saṅgraham evāpi sampaśhyan kartum arhasi (3.20)

King Janak and others attained perfection of Self-realization by selfless service (Karma Yoga) alone. You should also perform your duty with a view to guide people, and for the welfare of the society. (3.20)

yad yad ācharati śhreṣhṭhas tat tad evetaro janaḥ
sa yat pramāṇaṁ kurute lokas tad anuvartate (3.21)

Because whatever noble persons do, others follow. Whatever standard they set up, the world follows. (3.21)

saktāḥ karmaṇyavidvānso yathā kurvanti bhārata
kuryād vidvāns tathāsaktaśh chikīrṣhur loka-saṅgraham (3.25)

As the ignorant work with attachment to the fruits of work, so the wise should work without attachment, for the welfare of the society. (3.25)

indriyasyendriyasyārthe rāga-dveṣhau vyavasthitau
tayor na vaśham āgachchhet tau hyasya paripanthinau (3.34)

Attachments and aversions for the sense objects remain in the senses. One should not come under the control of these two, because they are two major stumbling blocks indeed, on one's path of Self-realization. (3.34)

śhreyān swa-dharmo viguṇaḥ para-dharmāt sv-anuṣhṭhitāt
swa-dharme nidhanaṁ śhreyaḥ para-dharmo bhayāvahaḥ (3.35)

One's inferior natural work is better than superior unnatural work. Death in carrying out one's natural work is useful. Unnatural work produces too much stress. (3.35)

Arjun uvācha
atha kena prayukto 'yaṁ pāpaṁ charati pūruṣhaḥ
anichchhann api vārṣhṇeya balād iva niyojitaḥ (3.36)

Arjun asked: O Krishna, what pushes a person to commit sin unwillingly as if forced against their will? (3.36)

Shrī Bhagavan uvācha
kāma eṣha krodha eṣha rajo-guṇa-samudbhavaḥ
mahāśhano mahā-pāpmā viddhyenam iha vairiṇam (3.37)

Krishna said: It is the desire born out of passion that becomes anger when unfulfilled. Desire is insatiable and is a great devil. Know this as the enemy. (3.37)

indriyāṇi parāṇyāhur indriyebhyaḥ paraṁ manaḥ
manasas tu parā buddhir yo buddheḥ paratas tu saḥ (3.42)

The senses are said to be superior to the body, the mind is superior to the senses, the intellect is superior to the mind, transcendental knowledge is superior to the intellect, and the Self is superior to transcendental knowledge. (3.42)

evaṁ buddheḥ paraṁ buddhvā sanstabhyātmānam ātmanā
jahi śhatruṁ mahā-bāho kāma-rūpaṁ durāsadam (3.43)

Thus, knowing the Self to be superior to the intellect, and controlling the mind by the intellect that is purified by spiritual practices, one must kill this mighty enemy, desire. (3.43)

Krishna had said that steady wisdom was freedom, which confused Arjun a bit, because to him fighting and killing people could not be wisdom.

"If you consider acquiring wisdom to be better than performing any action for a reason, then why do you want me to fight this terrible war?" he asked.

Krishna explained to Arjun that there are two kinds of people in the world, contemplative or introverts and the action-oriented people or extroverts.

"The introverts may not seem physically active, but their minds are always active, thinking and planning. Thought is an activity too. So, in effect, nobody is inactive or action-less. In fact, even the seemingly inactive nature around us is also constantly growing actively."

"All living beings are created from one source, the universal soul or cosmic intelligence. All are given divine wisdom and the universe functions smoothly because all are doing their duty selflessly."

Since we enjoy the bounties of universe, the life-giving sun, the nourishing rains and the food-giving earth, we should also do our part equally selflessly. Every activity is like a *yagya*, a give-and-get activity. What we sow, so we shall reap.

"The wise strive for wise action with steady determination. Such an action is Karma Yoga, in which one acts out of duty only, without any personal attachment or expectation."

Krishna reminded Arjun that our happiness comes only from right actions. And what is 'right action'? It is doing our duty selflessly. Arjun's duty as a warrior was to protect the righteous, the good people, even if he were to die in the war doing so.

Krishna then gave the example of King Janak in Ramayana.

"The great King Janak of Ayodhya performed his duty towards his kingdom very efficiently yet remained unattached to it all. His people considered him to be a saint. A true Karma Yogi always shows the way by personal example."

Arjun was listening to Krishna patiently. At times he understood what he said, but at times he looked puzzled.

"Sometimes I fail to understand your words, Krishna. On one hand you say that all emotions and attachments should be abandoned and on the other you are urging me to fight a battle that involves a lot of passion and anger, since I would be fighting with my own relatives. It sounds contradictory!"

Krishna clarified, "Everyone has to engage themselves in work which is suited to their natural skills or qualities they are born with. You were born a warrior, so your work is to fight. Work is neither good nor bad, it just *is*. The key is, that you must do your work selflessly, without any attachment to the task, to the people involved, or to the outcome. Loving or hating work are equally wrong, as they cause confusion in the mind, pushing you on the wrong path."

"Tell me then, Krishna, why do some people do terrible things, even when they know it is wrong? What forces a person to commit sin?" asked Arjun.

"Desire, dear Arjun, is our enemy that brings our downfall. It invites worries, sadness and suffering along with it. Unfulfilled desire gives rise to anger, which prevents us from seeing the soul or God within us or around us. Just as smoke hides the flame, our desire blocks our vision and confuses us, making us do all the wrong things. Kill this enemy called desire and be free from your confusion, my friend!" Krishna pushed his friend yet again.

How to do it?

Krishna explained that we, our physical bodies, are controlled by our five senses of taste, touch, sight, smell and sound, just like a chariot being pulled by five horses. But then, our mind is superior to our senses, and our intellect is superior to our mind.

We have to use our intellect as a charioteer to guide the reins of our mind in controlling the galloping horses of our desires, so they avoid falling prey to the temptations on the way. When that happens, the chariot, which is our body, starts moving on the right path in the right direction.

"O Kunti-putra, it is up to you to use your intellect to protect you from falling into the trap of desires," Krishna concluded.

After all, if the chariot meets with an accident, it's not the horses who would be blamed, but the charioteer!

It is better to face the struggles of life as a Karma Yogi instead of running away to lead a life of a false ascetic mentally engaged in worldly problems.

A very popular Puranic story illustrates this point. It goes like this...

Tavrit and Suvrit were two brothers who had left home in search of divine wisdom. They spent most of their time listening to learned *brahmins* in temples and mendicants passing through the city.

Once the brothers were going to a temple, when suddenly, it began raining heavily. They ran into the nearest building for shelter and discovered that it was a place where women danced to entertain their guests. Tavrit, the elder one, was appalled and walked out into the rain, to go to the temple. The younger brother, Suvrit, saw no harm in sitting there for a while to escape getting wet in the rain.

Tavrit reached the temple and sat listening to a discourse, but his mind was distracted. 'This is so boring! I should have remained with my brother. He must be enjoying himself, I'm sure. I made a mistake indeed!'

Suvrit, on the other hand, was also thinking. 'Why did I remain in this house of sin? My brother is so holy. He must be enjoying the wise *pandit's* discourse at the moment. I should have also braved the rain. I made a mistake indeed!'

The rain stopped and the brothers started out in the direction of the other. The moment they met, lightning struck them, and they died instantly. The *Yamdoot* took Tavrit to hell.

"I think you have made a mistake!" Tavrit exclaimed. "It was my brother who was sitting at the dance-house a little while ago. You should actually be taking him to hell."

The *Yamdoot* replied, "There has been no mistake. Your brother was sitting there to avoid the rain, but his heart was longing to be at the temple. On the other hand, while you were sitting and listening to the wise *pandit's* discourse at the temple, your heart was longing to be at the dance-house."

Tavrit had physically renounced the material world but was still attached to it in his mind. Such false renunciation is of no use. It is a waste of time.

4

Krishna explains GYAN YOGA

Krishna reveals the origin of divine knowledge to Arjun and discloses the reason for his own descension. He explains that though God is unborn and eternal, he descends to earth from time to time in human form to set things right. Krishna then elaborates the three kinds of nature of action, *attached, detached* and *forbidden* action. Those who do detached or selfless action, acquire Self-knowledge, which burns up all their past Karma and frees them from the cycle of birth and death.

Shrī Bhagavan uvācha
imaṁ vivasvate yogaṁ proktavān aham avyayam
vivasvān manave prāha manur ikṣhvākave 'bravīt (4.01)
evaṁ paramparā-prāptam imaṁ rājarṣhayo viduḥ

sa kāleneha mahatā yogo nașhțaḥ parantapa (4.02)
sa evāyaṁ mayā te 'dya yogaḥ proktaḥ purātanaḥ
bhakto 'si me sakhā cheti rahasyaṁ hyetad uttamam (4.03

Krishna said: I taught this Karma Yoga, the eternal science of right action, to King Vivasvan. Vivasvan taught it to Manu. Manu taught it to Ikshvaku. Thus handed down in succession the saintly kings knew this science of proper action. After a long time, this science was lost from this earth. Today I have described the same ancient science to you, because you are my sincere devotee and friend. This science is a supreme secret indeed. (4.01-03)

Arjun uvācha
aparaṁ bhavato janma paraṁ janma vivasvataḥ
katham etad vijānīyāṁ tvam ādau proktavān iti (4.04)

Arjun said: You were born later, but Vivasvan was born in ancient time. How am I to understand that you taught this science in the beginning of the creation? (4.04)

Shrī Bhagavan uvācha
bahūni me vyatītāni janmāni tava chārjuna
tānyahaṁ veda sarvāṇi na tvaṁ vettha parantapa (4.05)

Krishna said: Both you and I have taken many births. I remember them all, O Arjun, but you do not remember. (4.05)

ajo 'pi sannavyayātmā bhūtānām īśhvaro 'pi san
prakṛitiṁ svām adhișhțhāya sambhavāmyātma-māyayā (4.06)

Though I am eternal, immutable, and the Lord of all beings, yet I manifest myself by controlling the material nature using my own divine potential energy (Maya). (4.06)

yadā yadā hi dharmasya glānir bhavati bhārata
abhyutthānam adharmasya tadātmānaṁ sṛijāmyaham (4.07)
paritrāṇāya sādhūnāṁ vināśhāya cha duṣhkṛitām
dharma-sansthāpanārthāya sambhavāmi yuge yuge (4.08)

Whenever there is a decline of Dharma (righteousness) and a predominance of Adharma (unrighteousness), then I manifest myself. I appear from time to time for protecting the good, for transforming the wicked, and for establishing world order (Dharma). (4.07-08)

janma karma cha me divyam evaṁ yo vetti tattvataḥ
tyaktvā dehaṁ punar janma naiti mām eti so 'rjuna (4.09)

The one who truly understands my transcendental appearance, and activities of creation, maintenance and dissolution, attains my supreme abode and is not born again after leaving this body. (4.09)

na māṁ karmāṇi limpanti na me karma-phale spṛihā
iti māṁ yo 'bhijānāti karmabhir na sa badhyate (4.14)

Works do not bind me, because I have no desire for the fruits of work. The one who fully understands and practices this truth is also not bound by Karma. (4.14)

karmaṇo hyapi boddhavyaṁ boddhavyaṁ cha vikarmaṇaḥ
akarmaṇaśh cha boddhavyaṁ gahanā karmaṇo gatiḥ (4.17)

The true nature of action is very difficult to understand. Therefore, one should know the nature of attached action, the nature of detached action, and also the nature of forbidden action. (4.17)

yathaidhānsi samiddho 'gnir bhasma-sāt kurute 'rjuna
jñānāgniḥ sarva-karmāṇi bhasma-sāt kurute tathā (4.37)

As the blazing fire reduces wood to ashes; similarly, the fire of Self-knowledge reduces all bonds of Karma to ashes. (4.37)

na hi jñānena sadṛiśhaṁ pavitramiha vidyate
tatsvayaṁ yogasansiddhaḥ kālenātmani vindati (4.38)

There is no purifier in this world like the true knowledge of the Supreme Being. One discovers this knowledge within, naturally, in course of time when one's mind is cleansed of selfishness by Karma Yoga. (4.38)

śhraddhāvānllabhate jñānaṁ tat-paraḥ sanyatendriyaḥ
jñānaṁ labdhvā parāṁ śhāntim achireṇādhigachchhati (4.39)

The one who has faith in God, is sincere in yogic practices, and has control over the mind and senses, gains this transcendental knowledge. Having gained this knowledge, one quickly attains supreme peace or liberation. (4.39)

yoga-sannyasta-karmāṇaṁ jñāna-sañchhinna-sanśhayam
ātmavantaṁ na karmāṇi nibadhnanti dhanañjaya (4.41)

Work does not bind a person who has renounced work by renouncing the fruits of work through Karma Yoga, and whose confusion regarding body and Spirit is completely destroyed by the application of Self-knowledge. (4.41)

tasmād ajñāna-sambhūtaṁ hṛit-sthaṁ jñānāsinātmanaḥ
chhittvainaṁ sanśhayaṁ yogam ātiṣhṭhottiṣhṭha bhārata (4.42)

Cut the ignorance-born confusion regarding body and Spirit by the sword of Self-knowledge, resort to Karma Yoga, and get up for the war. (4.42)

Krishna revealed a stunning fact about himself. "The divine knowledge, the secret of happiness, of doing your work selflessly with no attachment to its fruit, is the eternal truth that I have been teaching since the beginning of time. I taught it to Vivasvan or Surya, who passed it on to Manu who shared it with Ikshvaku, the first king of the solar dynasty, and so on."

As was expected, Arjun was shocked. "You were born much later than Vivasvan, so how could you do that!" he exclaimed.

Krishna smiled at his friend's look of disbelief and said, "Like me, you too have lived many lives before this one. It is just that I remember them all, while you don't. I don't need to be born, Arjun, as I am the Lord of all creatures, who is never born and never dies. But I choose to be born on earth, every now and then."

Why? Before Arjun could ask the question, Krishna continued, "Whenever there is a decline in righteousness in the world and rise in the evil, I manifest myself for the protection of the good and destruction of the evildoers. I am reborn throughout the ages to ensure that righteousness returns to the world. Those who understand this divine truth, become free from fear, desire and anger. This wisdom, the knowledge of God, burns away all doubts. Even if you are the most sinful person, you can burn all the sins with knowledge. Knowledge is a purifier."

Arjun could now begin to understand that when a person realizes the impermanent nature of things around him, including his own self, all his desires naturally fall away from him, leaving him free and at peace.

"Since everything is impermanent anyway, why kill at all! How can the action of killing be good?" Arjun returned to his original problem.

"No action in itself is good or bad, it is the intent behind it which is. When you, your kingdom, your people are attacked by someone, a war is declared. Is it not your responsibility to protect your people? How will you do it if you don't fight back the attackers? Yes, people will be killed. But your fighting for the right cause, to protect your kingdom and people, to bring back righteousness to the world, is a good action."

Krishna had grabbed Arjun's attention, so he continued, "Killing is a *forbidden* action. It is sinful. When killing happens for a reason, like winning a war, it becomes *attached* action, as the desire of winning is attached to it. It becomes personal. And that is dangerous, because if the desire is not fulfilled, the person will get angry and may do something worse. But when killing has no personal reason, when it happens like a side effect of a war, when the result is the larger benefit of people, when winning or losing does not personally affect the person, then it is a *detached* action. The person is just a doer, he is doing his duty to the best of his ability."

Krishna explained that when we choose an action, we also choose its result. That is why work, or any action has to be done for the welfare of all and not just to satisfy a desire or personal gain. Such selfless action is Karma Yoga.

"Whatever work a person may do, whether it is teaching, trading, tilling land or fighting against injustice, his action should be right. Right action is that which is done without desire of reward or fear of failure, it is done like a sacrifice."

"Sacrifice! How can an action be done like a sacrifice?" shot out the obvious question from Arjun.

"Sacrifice does not mean offering of money or material things. It means offering yourself. Some people sacrifice the pleasures of their senses and withdraw from the material world. Some enjoy being in the material world, accepting everything as a gift from universe but not claiming anything for themselves, which is their sacrifice. Some do arduous physical pilgrimages, sacrificing their comfort. Some do regular fasting, sacrificing their hunger. Some give regular donations to the needy, sacrificing their money. People do different sacrifices to discipline their bodies and control their minds, because they understand that self-discipline brings divine wisdom."

This was certainly a new way of looking at any action, Arjun thought to himself.

"Ignorance gives rise to doubts, destroy it with your sword of knowledge. Have faith in your right action and sacrifice your fears and doubts to me. Stand up O Arjun and fight!"

Krishna was trying to make Arjun understand the importance of divine knowledge and how by using it one is able to do detached action and be free from the cycle of birth and death. According to him, it is the state of mind of the doer that determines whether their action is attached or detached.

There's a story in the Puranas about it...

Once the cowherd women of Vrindavan kept a fast. The ceremony of breaking the fast required them to feed a sage. Krishna advised them to feed sage Durvasa, who lived on the banks of river Yamuna, right across from where they lived.

The women happily prepared an elaborate meal for the sage and went to meet him, carrying several baskets of delicious food.

Durvasa, being a sage, lived a frugal life and ate very little. Seeing the disappointed faces of the women when he took a small portion of the food, Durvasa decided to fulfil their expectations. Using his mystic powers, he ate everything they had brought. And it was quite a lot! The women were amazed, and pleased as well, to see that the sage had done justice to their food.

Finally, taking sage Durvasa's blessings and empty food baskets, the women set off for home. But when they reached the riverbank, they were disappointed to find that no boatman was willing to take them across. Actually, the weather was windy, and the river had become quite turbulent. The women went back to sage Durvasa to seek help.

He told them to request river Yamuna to give way, by saying that if sage Durvasa has not eaten anything today, except *doob* grass, then the river should give way to them. Considering that the women had seen the sage having a substantial meal, the idea sounded crazy. But, having no choice, the women did as they were told. Lo and behold...the great river Yamuna parted for the women to walk across!

The women went to Krishna to find out the cause of this magical phenomena. He heard their story and smiled. Then he explained, "When the sages appear to be doing material activities externally, internally they are not involved in the activity at all. They function in a detached manner. So, for sage Durvasa, eating delicious food and *doob* grass are the same. He is attached to neither."

5

Krishna explains RENUNCIATION

Arjun is still confused about whether renunciation of work is better or selfless work. Krishna explains that selfless work without attachment to its results is better for most people. He also explains that *sannyas* or renunciation does not mean leaving worldly possessions. It means not being attached to them. Finally, Krishna describes how a Karma Yogi is always in a state of peace, since his mind and senses are in his own control. Such a person sees God in all beings and treats everybody equally.

Arjun uvācha
sannyāsaṁ karmaṇāṁ Krishna punar yogaṁ cha śhansasi
yach chhreya etayor ekaṁ tan me brūhi su-niśhchitam (5.01)

Arjun asked: O Krishna, you praised the path of sacrificing action, and also the path of performance of selfless action.

Please tell me decisively which of the two is better. (5.01)

Shrī Bhagavan uvācha
sannyāsaḥ karma-yogaśh cha niḥśhreyasa-karāvubhau
tayos tu karma-sannyāsāt karma-yogo viśhiṣhyate (5.02)

Krishna said: The path of Self-knowledge and the path of selfless service both lead to the supreme goal. But of the two, the path of selfless service is superior to path of Self-knowledge, because it is easier to practice. (5.02)

yat sānkhyaiḥ prāpyate sthānaṁ tad yogair api gamyate
ekaṁ sānkhyaṁ cha yogaṁ cha yaḥ paśhyati sa paśhyati (5.05)

Whatever goal a renunciate reaches, a Karma Yogi also reaches the same goal. Therefore, the one who sees the path of renunciation and the path of selfless work as the same, really sees. (5.05)

sannyāsas tu mahā-bāho duḥkham āptum ayogataḥ
yoga-yukto munir brahma na chireṇādhigachchhati (5.06)

True renunciation of action is difficult to attain without performance of action. A sage devoted to action quickly attains Nirvana. (5.06)

brahmaṇyādhāya karmāṇi saṅgaṁ tyaktvā karoti yaḥ
lipyate na sa pāpena padma-patram ivāmbhasā (5.10)

One who does all work as an offering to God—abandoning selfish attachment to results—remains untouched by Karmic reaction or sin as a lotus never gets wet by water. (5.10)

yuktaḥ karma-phalaṁ tyaktvā śhāntim āpnoti naiṣhṭhikīm
ayuktaḥ kāma-kāreṇa phale sakto nibadhyate (5.12)

A Karma Yogi attains unshakable peace by abandoning attachment to the fruits of work; while others, who are attached to the fruits of work, become bound by selfish work. (5.12)

vidyā-vinaya-sampanne brāhmaṇe gavi hastini
śhuni chaiva śhva-pāke cha paṇḍitāḥ sama-darśhinaḥ
(5.18)

An enlightened person—by perceiving God in all—looks at a learned person, an outcast, even a cow, an elephant, or a dog in the same way. (5.18)

na prahṛiṣhyet priyaṁ prāpya nodvijet prāpya chāpriyam
sthira-buddhir asammūḍho brahma-vid brahmaṇi sthitaḥ
(5.20)

One who neither rejoices on obtaining what is pleasant, nor grieves on obtaining the unpleasant, who has a steady mind, who is not deluded, and who is a knower of the Supreme Being, such a person eternally abides with the Supreme Being. (5.20)

ye hi sansparśha-jā bhogā duḥkha-yonaya eva te
ādyantavantaḥ kaunteya na teṣhu ramate budhaḥ (5.22)

Sensual pleasures are verily the source of misery and have a beginning and an end. Therefore, the wise do not rejoice in sensual pleasures. (5.22)

bhoktāraṁ yajña-tapasāṁ sarva-loka-maheśhvaram
suhṛidaṁ sarva-bhūtānāṁ jñātvā māṁ śhāntim ṛichchhati
(5.29)

A true yogi observes me in all beings and also sees every being in me. Indeed, the Self-realized person sees me, the same Supreme Lord, everywhere. (5.29)

Arjun wondered that since according to Krishna sacrifice is so important, would it not be better to sacrifice the glory of winning the war by sacrificing the very idea of fighting the war?

"I feel that sacrificing might be a better option than to fight selflessly. At least I won't have to kill my kith and kin," he said to Krishna.

"Both the paths of sacrificing action and selfless action lead to wisdom and happiness in life, but the second one is better and doable by most people," Krishna responded instantly.

Since his childhood, Arjun had learnt that the path of sages, the *sannyasis*, was very noble, since they sacrificed their worldly pleasures and spent their entire lives in praying and meditating. Krishna seemed to be saying something contradictory! According to him, the path of selfless action was better than that of sacrificing one's material possessions.

"If someone's material sacrifice is not connected to any spiritual cause, then such sacrifice becomes simply materialistic. But if one performs sacrifice with a spiritual objective, then he makes a perfect sacrifice. Whereas selfless action means that one does his work without desiring anything from it nor rejecting anything about it. Such a person is a *sannyasi* while still fulfilling his duties. A wise person understands that the paths of selfless action and renunciation are the same," Krishna elaborated patiently.

"If I walk away from this battle, would it not be renunciation then? Am I not being selfless, when I say I do not desire to win or rule the kingdom?" Arjun had his own point of view.

"Renunciation does not mean walking away from action. What you are saying you want to do is *inaction*. It is called rejection of action, and rejection is a selfish action. Walking away is a cowardly action, an irresponsible action, which is just the opposite of selfless action. You have to learn the right inaction, which is inaction in action," Krishna clarified.

Right inaction! Arjun had heard about right action, but this?

Krishna continued, "When a person is able to be completely involved in action with his body and his senses, while being completely steeped in inaction at his core, his soul will remain undisturbed. Such a person neither expects rewards nor fears the results of his action; his soul is neither attached to nor rejects the action. This is inaction of mind, the right inaction."

Arjun mulled over what Krishna said. A true *sannyasi* according to Krishna was one who fulfilled his responsibilities without craving reward or fearing punishment. Though what he said made sense, but it was still not easy to remain undisturbed at the core while killing people.

As though reading Arjun's mind, Krishna went on, "A Karma Yogi neither rejoices when something pleasant happens nor grieves when something unpleasant does, because he is not attached to the fruits of his action."

"He is never attracted to the temptations the world throws at him, because he has his senses under control. Sensual pleasures are the root cause of all misery. A wise person is aware that all pain and pleasure come from things that appeal to the senses, and that is the main cause of all anger and sorrow. He is also aware that such pleasures end soon. He is never confused because he has his mind under control. Controlling of mind is the key, Parth." Krishna paused.

"Abandon all attachments and be like a lotus. Though floating in muddy water, the lotus remains unsoiled."

A lotus grows from the mud at the bottom of the pond or lake, yet it rises above the water and blossoms towards the sun. It has large leaves that also float on the surface of water. These large leaves are waterproof, any liquid poured over them does not get absorbed but runs off. Hence, they are also used as plates by some people. Krishna's example shows that although the lotus owes its birth, growth and sustenance to water, its leaf does not permit itself to be wetted.

This is how a wise man lives in the material world, unaffected by sensory temptations.

"A person with inner peace sees me in all creatures, be that a learned man or a fool, be a cow, an elephant, or a dog, and he treats them all in the same manner. He sees me everywhere, in everything, knowing that I am the Lord of all the worlds. He trusts me completely. He offers his work as a sacrifice to me and thus remains inactive at the core while in action. O Kaunteya, this is what you have to do," concluded Krishna.

When we accept everything as the will of God, we lead a peaceful and happy life.

There is an old fable in this context—the origin of this little story is unknown, but all fables, from whichever part of the world they might be, are a reflection of universal ancient wisdom.

Once a wild horse entered a farm. The farmer took the wild beast in and fed him. The neighbours congratulated the farmer on his good luck. "Good luck, bad luck, who knows! It's all God's will," was his response. A few days later, the horse ran away. The farmer's neighbours sympathized with him, feeling sorry for his bad luck. "Good luck, bad luck, who knows! It's all God's will," was the farmer's response this time too.

After some time, the wild horse returned with twenty more wild horses. Again, the people rushed to congratulate the farmer on his good luck. And again, his response was, "Good luck, bad luck, who knows! It's all God's will." Sometime later, the farmer's son broke his leg while riding one of the horses. The farmer's friends expressed their grief on his bad luck. The farmer of course had the same response, "Good luck, bad luck, who knows! It's all God's will."

One day, the king's men visited the farmer's neighbourhood and recruited all the young men into the royal army. The farmer's son was spared because of his broken leg. People called this the farmer's good luck. But the farmer still maintained his stance about life, "Good luck, bad luck, who knows! It's all God's will."

Such equanimity is possible only when we are emotionally detached from the material world, like a lotus.

6

Krishna explains DHYAN YOGA

After divine knowledge and selfless work, Krishna shows the third path to peace and happiness to Arjun—the path of meditation. He emphasizes the importance of self-discipline or yoga. A real yogi works according to his prescribed duty, without attachment to results or a desire for sense gratification. This is achieved with the help of a controlled mind. By regulation of eating, sleeping, work, and recreation, the yogi gains control over his body, mind and activities, and becomes steady in his meditation.

Shrī Bhagavan uvācha
yaṁ sannyāsam iti prāhur yogaṁ taṁ viddhi pāṇḍava
na hyasannyasta-saṅkalpo yogī bhavati kaśhchana (6.02)

Krishna said: Renunciation is same as Karma Yoga. Because no one becomes a Karma Yogi who has not renounced the selfish motive behind an action. (6.02)

uddhared ātmanātmānaṁ nātmānam avasādayet
ātmaiva hyātmano bandhur ātmaiva ripur ātmanaḥ (6.05)
bandhur ātmātmanas tasya yenātmaivātmanā jitaḥ
anātmanas tu śhatrutve vartetātmaiva śhatru-vat (6.06)

One must elevate, and not degrade oneself by one's own mind. The mind is one's friend as well as one's enemy. The mind is the friend of those who have control over it, and the mind acts like an enemy for those who do not control it. (6.05-06)

jñāna-vijñāna-tṛiptātmā kūṭa-stho vijitendriyaḥ
yukta ityuchyate yogī sama-loṣhṭāśhma-kāñchanaḥ (6.08)

A person is called yogi who has both Self-knowledge and Self-realization, who is equanimous, who has control over the mind and senses, and to whom a clod of earth, a stone, and gold is the same. (6.08)

suhṛin-mitrāryudāsīna-madhyastha-dveṣhya-bandhuṣhu
sādhuṣhvapi cha pāpeṣhu sama-buddhir viśhiṣhyate (6.09)

A person is considered superior who is impartial towards companions, friends, enemies, neutrals, arbiters, haters, relatives, saints, and sinners. (6.09)

yathā dīpo nivāta-stho neṅgate sopamā smṛitā
yogino yata-chittasya yuñjato yogam ātmanaḥ (6.19)

A lamp, in a place sheltered by the Spirit from the wind of desires, does not flicker. This simile is used for the subdued mind of a yogi practising meditation on the Spirit. (6.19)

Arjun uvācha
yo 'yaṁ yogas tvayā proktaḥ sāmyena Madhusudan
etasyāhaṁ na paśhyāmi chañchalatvāt sthitiṁ sthirām (6.33)
chañchalaṁ hi manaḥ Krishna pramāthi balavad dṛiḍham
tasyāhaṁ nigrahaṁ manye vāyor iva su-duṣhkaram (6.34)

Arjun said: O Krishna, You have said that the yoga of meditation is characterized by the equanimity of mind, but due to restlessness of mind I do not perceive the steady state of mind. Because the mind, indeed, is very unsteady, turbulent, powerful, and obstinate, O Krishna. I think restraining the mind is as difficult as restraining the wind. (6.33-34)

ayatiḥ śhraddhayopeto yogāch chalita-mānasaḥ
aprāpya yoga-sansiddhiṁ kāṅ gatiṁ Krishna gachchhati (6.37)

The faithful who deviates from the path of meditation and fails to attain yogic perfection due to unsubdued mind — what is the destination of such a person, O Krishna? (6.37)

Shrī Bhagavan uvācha
prāpya puṇya-kṛitāṁ lokān uṣhitvā śhāśhvatīḥ samāḥ
śhuchīnāṁ śhrīmatāṁ gehe yoga-bhraṣhṭo 'bhijāyate (6.41)
atha vā yoginām eva kule bhavati dhīmatām
etad dhi durlabhataraṁ loke janma yad īdṛiśham (6.42)

Krishna said: The less evolved unsuccessful yogi is reborn in the house of the pious and prosperous after attaining heaven and living there for many years. The highly evolved unsuccessful yogi does not go to heaven, but is born in a spiritually advanced family. A birth like this is very difficult, indeed, to obtain in this world. (6.41-42)

yoginām api sarveṣhāṁ mad-gatenāntar-ātmanā
śhraddhāvān bhajate yo māṁ sa me yuktatamo mataḥ
(6.47)

I consider the yogi-devotee who lovingly contemplates on me with supreme faith, and whose mind is ever absorbed in me to be the best of all the yogis. (6.47)

Krishna wanted Arjun to understand that renouncing the war was not selfless for him. In fact, it was the other way round. Arjun's leaving the battlefield would not have stopped the war. His brothers would continue to fight and probably get killed without Arjun's leadership.

"The real meaning of renunciation is abandoning the selfish motive behind any action. It is not the action but the motive which is more important. When action or work is done selflessly, it purifies the mind," Krishna explained.

"The main thing is discipline, self-discipline. It results in disciplined action. Doing an action or work you are meant to do, in a detached and disciplined manner, is Karma Yoga or the yoga of action. Likewise, doing spiritual study in a detached and disciplined manner is Gyan Yoga or the yoga of knowledge. Both the paths lead to wisdom," he said.

As a warrior, Arjun understood about physical discipline and training in warfare. But mental discipline was new to him.

Krishna explained how it was important to engage one's body, mind and soul in the service of God. The mind is the most difficult to control and one has to conquer it, otherwise, lust, anger, greed, hatred, etc. would always distract and deviate the person from the right path. The conqueror of mind automatically follows the direction of the Supreme-soul or God.

"How should one control one's mind, Krishna?" was the expected question from Arjun.

"One can control it through meditation. The third path to divine wisdom or God is the yoga of meditation or Dhyan Yoga," was Krishna's response. "But this also needs to be done in a detached and disciplined manner."

Yoga is the union of a person's soul with the universal energy source, or God. It is achieved by focussing on the source and stilling the mind. A self-disciplined person is called a *yogi*. He has control over his mind, senses and desires. He is free from anger and greed. He sees God in everything and everything in God.

Krishna then described the basic meditation technique to Arjun.

"The yogis conquer the mind through meditation, because a trained mind is our best friend, and an untrained mind can be our worst enemy. Meditation is a way for uniting the mind with God, and it is not difficult at all. In order to meditate, sitting in a quiet place, one should hold one's spine, neck and head erect and stare steadily at the tip of one's nose. Then, with a calm mind, one should focus on one's innermost soul or God, which is me. This should be done regularly, because only through practice does one learn to do a thing well."

Meditation teaches us to focus on one point. And in doing so, while observing the movement of our own breath, our thoughts fall away. This should be the state of our mind at all times. It's an ideal state, where undisturbed by worldly attachments, we move on towards eternal peace. When we observe the flow of our own breath, we realize it's the same breath that flows through every living being. And once we understand that, we treat all living beings the same way. This is real *yoga*.

"It sounds so simple, but is it so?" Arjun wondered.

Krishna smiled indulgently. "Similar to a lamp that does not flicker in a windless place, a *yogi's* mind is steady in meditation. I agree, it is difficult to control the mind, but it can be done by practice and detachment. Whenever your mind wanders away, you need to bring it back and continue to focus on God."

He cautioned Arjun that merely doing meditation is not enough, a *yogi* has to look after his body too. The basic necessities like food, sleep, work, and recreation need to be regulated and moderated. Moderation is the first step towards discipline. Continuous practice of this results in controlling the senses and desires better.

"When the mind is still, and the desires are in control, can a person experience the happiness within his heart. Such a person can never be sad anymore, as he can see the true nature of the world. He sees himself in everything around him and that oneness gives him eternal peace," said Krishna.

"What happens to those spiritual aspirants who begin their journey, but due to an unsteady mind, are unable to reach their goal?" Arjun wanted to know.

"Nothing!" was Krishna's instant response. "Such a man will be born again in a family of *yogis*, where he would resume his practice from where he left off in the earlier life. Nothing goes waste!"

"A true *yogi* is superior to a *sannyasi*, to a scholar, and even a disciplined worker. With a heart full of faith and devotion for me, pick up your bow and be a *yogi*, Arjun," Krishna declared.

When we talk of being a *yogi*, one name immediately comes to mind, it's that of Dhruv. He was the son of King Uttanapada and Queen Suniti. The king had another wife, Suruchi, and a son, Uttam, from her. Unfortunately, the king was partial towards Suruchi and Uttam and neglected Suniti and Dhruv completely.

One day, the king was sitting on the throne and little Uttam was playing on his lap. Five-year-old Dhruv saw this and wanted to do the same as his stepbrother. But his stepmother intervened. She said, "If you want to sit on your father's lap, you should have been born to me and not to Suniti. Go and pray to God to make your wish come true."

Little Dhruv felt bad and went crying to his mother. Suniti consoled her son and told him to take Suruchi's words seriously. She told him to pray to Vishnu, who helps everyone. Dhruv left home and headed towards the forest to find a place to pray to Vishnu.

The little boy's aim was to reach a place higher than the king's throne. He wanted people to look up to him, as they looked up to the king for guidance. Dhruv believed that Vishnu could help him reach that place. On the way, he met sage Narad, who was an ardent devotee of Vishnu. The sage gave Dhruv a mantra to chant as prayer.

So powerful was little Dhruv's meditation that the earth began to shake! Suniti rushed to meet Dhruv. Seeing him engrossed in his meditation, she began to worry for his health, as he was merely a five-year-old child. She told him to stop everything and return to his normal life, but Dhruv was totally absorbed in his prayers. He was oblivious to his surroundings. Suniti returned.

Ultimately, pleased with the little boy's devotion, Vishnu appeared before him. He blessed Dhruv and promised that he would attain his desire to be at a

place much higher that the royal throne. "I will grant you a fixed position in the northern sky that is far above the sun, moon, planets and all the constellations. People will look up to you with the faith that you will show them the right direction."

Dhruv became *Dhruv Tara* or the fixed pole-star, that we see shining in the northern sky, a star that is used to finding direction, and navigation.

Such is the power of meditation.

7

Krishna explains ULTIMATE WISDOM

Krishna reveals himself as the origin of all material and spiritual energies. He explains that like beads strung on a single thread, all these energies have originated from him and rest in him. The entire creation begins from and dissolves into him. There is only one God, Krishna. Devas, devis, and other deities are just the names of different powers of that one God.

Shrī Bhagavan uvācha
mayyāsakta-manāḥ Parth yogaṁ yuñjan mad-āśhrayaḥ
asanśhayaṁ samagraṁ māṁ yathā jñāsyasi tach chhṛiṇu
(7.01)

Krishna said: Now listen, O Arjun, how, with the mind attached exclusively to me and surrendering to me through the practice of bhakti yoga, you can know me fully without any doubt. (7.01)

jñānaṁ te 'haṁ sa-vijñānam idaṁ vakṣhyāmyaśheṣhataḥ
yaj jñātvā neha bhūyo 'nyaj jñātavyam-avaśhiṣhyate (7.02)

I shall now fully reveal unto you this knowledge and wisdom, knowing which nothing else remains to be known in this world. (7.02)

manuṣhyāṇāṁ sahasreṣhu kaśhchid yatati siddhaye
yatatām api siddhānāṁ kaśhchin māṁ vetti tattvataḥ (7.03)

Amongst thousands of persons, hardly one strives for perfection; and amongst those who have achieved perfection, hardly one knows me in truth. (7.03)

bhūmir-āpo 'nalo vāyuḥ khaṁ mano buddhir eva cha
ahankāra itīyaṁ me bhinnā prakṛitir aṣhṭadhā (7.04)

The mind, intellect, ego, ether, air, fire, water, and earth are the eightfold division of my nature. (7.04)

apareyam itas tvanyāṁ prakṛitiṁ viddhi me parām
jīva-bhūtāṁ mahā-bāho yayedaṁ dhāryate jagat (7.05)

The material nature or Matter is my lower nature. My higher nature is the Spirit by which this entire universe is sustained. (7.05)

etad-yonīni bhūtāni sarvāṇītyupadhāraya
ahaṁ kṛitsnasya jagataḥ prabhavaḥ pralayas tathā (7.06)

Know that all creatures have evolved from this twofold energy; and the Supreme Spirit is the source of origin as well as dissolution of the entire universe. (7.06)

mattaḥ parataraṁ nānyat kiñchid asti dhanañjaya
mayi sarvam idaṁ protaṁ sūtre maṇi-gaṇā iva (7.07)

There is nothing higher than the Supreme Being. Everything in the universe is strung on the Supreme Being, like jewels are strung on the thread of a necklace. (7.07)

ye chaiva sāttvikā bhāvā rājasās tāmasāśh cha ye
matta eveti tān viddhi na tvahaṁ teṣhu te mayi (7.12)

Know that the three modes of material nature, goodness, passion, and ignorance, also emanate from me. I am not dependent on, or affected by, the modes of material nature; but the modes of material nature are dependent on me. (7.12)

tribhir guṇa-mayair bhāvair ebhiḥ sarvam idaṁ jagat
mohitaṁ nābhijānāti māmebhyaḥ param avyayam (7.13)

Human beings are deluded by various aspects of these three modes of material nature; therefore, they do not know me, who is eternal and above these modes. (7.13)

chatur-vidhā bhajante māṁ janāḥ sukṛitino 'rjuna
ārto jijñāsur arthārthī jñānī cha bharatarṣhabha (7.16)

Four types of virtuous ones worship or seek me. They are: the distressed, the seeker of Self-knowledge, the seeker of wealth, and the enlightened one who has experienced the Supreme Being. (7.16)

yo yo yāṁ yāṁ tanuṁ bhaktaḥ śhraddhayārchitum ichchhati
tasya tasyāchalāṁ śhraddhāṁ tām eva vidadhāmyaham (7.21)

sa tayā śhraddhayā yuktas tasyārādhanam īhate
labhate cha tataḥ kāmān mayaiva vihitān hi tān (7.22)

Whosoever desires to worship whatever deity—using any name, form, and method—with faith, I make their faith steady in that very deity. Endowed with steady faith they worship that deity and obtain their wishes through that deity. Those wishes are granted by me. (7.21-22)

avyaktaṁ vyaktim āpannaṁ manyante mām abuddhayaḥ
paraṁ bhāvam ajānanto mamāvyayam anuttamam (7.24)
nāhaṁ prakāśhaḥ sarvasya yoga-māyā-samāvṛitaḥ
mūḍho 'yaṁ nābhijānāti loko mām ajam avyayam (7.25)

The ignorant ones, unable to understand my immutable, incomparable, incomprehensible, and transcendental form, assume that I, the Supreme Being, am formless and take forms or incarnate. Concealed by my divine power (Maya), I do not reveal myself to such deluded ones. (7.24-25)

sādhibhūtādhidaivaṁ māṁ sādhiyajñaṁ cha ye viduḥ
prayāṇa-kāle 'pi cha māṁ te vidur yukta-chetasaḥ (7.30)

The wise ones, who know me alone as the basis of all the mortal beings, temporal beings, and the eternal being even at the time of death, attain me. (7.30)

Krishna spoke about meditating on the innermost soul, the eternal spirit or God. But how should one worship him and meditate upon him? These were some of the questions bothering Arjun.

So, Krishna decided to impart the ultimate divine knowledge regarding God to his dear friend, which would result in him acquiring ultimate wisdom.

"Very few people try to understand my true nature, they mostly go through life following what others are doing without ever wondering why they are doing so. Out of the few who try to understand me, hardly one succeeds. But today, I will explain my true nature to you, my friend, so that all your doubts disappear."

"The entire creation is made up of five basic elements in different proportions. The elements are earth, water, fire, air and space. Other than these, mind, intellect and ego are three more elements that are present in a human being. As everything else, the five natural and the three subtle elements are the manifestation of God, or me."

There are two kinds of nature of God, the first one is Matter, which is his lower nature. The second or the higher nature is the Spirit (soul), without which the Matter remains inert. Matter, also known as Prakriti, is inert, while the Spirit, also known as Purush, is dynamic. A combination of Matter and Spirit causes things to be born and function.

Matter or Prakriti on its own cannot generate anything. The Spirit therefore is the cause of creation and dissolution of the universe. But then, someone has to direct what to create and what to dissolve. That power is called God, the supreme being or the eternal soul. So, it is God who decides to put the Spirit or consciousness into Matter resulting in the creation of the universe or taking the Spirit away from Matter resulting in the dissolution of the universe.

"There is a huge variety of living beings in the universe, all carrying the same eternal soul or God. It is like a variety of beads strung together, supported by one string, to form a necklace. I am that string who supports the entire universe," said Krishna.

Arjun's gaze remained transfixed on Krishna as he explained that he is the essence of everything—the taste of water, the heat in fire, the sound in ether, the light of the sun and the moon, the ability in man, the original fragrance of the earth, the intelligence of the intelligent, and the life of all that lives.

"But what about the all the bad things around us?" Arjun wanted to know.

"Yes, those too. A person's darkest thoughts or his ignorance also come from me, as well as his goodness and intelligence. In fact, every changing mood of a person, every aspect of his contradictory behaviour, comes from me."

How?

"The three states of material existence, creation, preservation and destruction, or the three *gunas* are manifested by my energy as *rajas*, *sattva* and *tamas*. *Rajas* leads to passionate action, *sattva* to goodness, balance and serenity, while *tamas* leads to ignorance and lethargy."

"But how is it that people do not see you as the supreme creator and controller of everything?" Arjun seemed genuinely perplexed.

"Most people are trapped in the web of their desires and are unable to see the truth. They seek God only when they are sick or in some kind of trouble or when they desire wealth. At the same time, there are some who are curious about God and seek to know more. But those who know about God and seek him without wanting anything for themselves are the best of the seekers."

"I see people worshipping different gods. Is that wrong then?" Arjun wanted to know.

"Not at all! I am the source of all that exists including the celestial gods. They derive their power from me. Whatever deity a person may choose to worship, the wishes are granted by me."

Krishna further continued, "The kind of thoughts one has during the course of his life, accumulate to influence his thoughts at the time of his death. Whatever state of being one is in at the time of death, he attains that without fail. The present life creates one's next life. So, one should always contemplate on God."

"How should a person do that?" asked Arjun.

"Simply by performing devotional service, it is easy for my devotees to attain me at the time of their death," Krishna replied.

According to a very popular folktale, long ago, there was a gurukul on the outskirts of a forest, where young boys lived and studied, just like in the hostels of today. Amongst other things, the students were taught to see God in all beings.

One day, as the young boys were collecting wood for fire, they heard loud trumpeting of an elephant and a man shouting, "A mad elephant is coming! Save yourselves!"

Naturally, the boys left everything and ran back to the ashram! But not all of them. One of the boys stayed back. He remained standing, with head bowed and hands folded.

The elephant was being followed by his mahout or trainer, who kept on shouting, "Get out of the way! The elephant has gone mad!"

The boy did not move. What happened next was expected. The elephant grabbed the boy with his trunk and threw him on one side and went on its way trumpeting loudly.

After the elephant left, the other boys rushed to the injured boy, to bring him back into the ashram. When the boy finally regained consciousness, they wanted to know why he stayed back when everyone else left the forest.

The young boy said, "Our guruji taught us that God is in all living beings, including plants and animals. Hence, I thought that it was an elephant-God who was coming. So, I stood and prayed."

Their guru heard this and laughed. "Yes, it was indeed the elephant-God coming. But why didn't you pay attention to the mahout-God who told you to get out of the way? The elephant-god does not have the divine knowledge that all beings are gods!"

God dwells in all beings, but each being has its own nature according to which they act. Respecting all beings is important, as is using one's common sense.

8

Krishna explains the ETERNAL SPIRIT

Krishna explains the cycle of creation and what decides the destiny of the soul after death. He also talks about transmigration of soul. Some important terms are explained. Krishna explains how beings manifest, and that at the time of dissolution, everything is absorbed back into him.

Arjun uvācha
kiṁ tad brahma kim adhyātmaṁ kiṁ karma puruṣhottama
adhibhūtaṁ cha kiṁ proktam adhidaivaṁ kim uchyate (8.01)
adhiyajñaḥ kathaṁ ko 'tra dehe 'smin Madhusudan
prayāṇa-kāle cha kathaṁ jñeyo 'si niyatātmabhiḥ (8.02)

Arjun asked: O Krishna, who is the eternal being or the Spirit? What is the nature of the eternal being? What is Karma?

Who are the mortal beings? And who are temporal beings? Who is the supreme being, and how does he dwell in the body? How can you, the supreme being, be remembered at the time of death by those who have control over their minds, O Krishna? (8.01-02)

Shrī Bhagavan uvācha
yaṁ yaṁ vāpi smaran bhāvaṁ tyajatyante kalevaram
taṁ tam evaiti kaunteya sadā tad-bhāva-bhāvitaḥ (8.06)

Krishna said: Remembering whatever object when one leaves the body at the end of life, one attains that object. Thought of whatever object prevails during one's lifetime, one remembers only that object at the end of life and achieves it. (8.06)

tasmāt sarveṣhu kāleṣhu mām anusmara yudhya cha
mayyarpita-mano-buddhir mām evaiṣhyasyasanśhayam (8.07)

Therefore, always remember me and do your duty. You shall certainly attain me if your mind and intellect are forever focused on me. (8.07)

sahasra-yuga-paryantam ahar yad brahmaṇo viduḥ
rātriṁ yuga-sahasrāntāṁ te 'ho-rātra-vido janāḥ (8.17)

Those who know that the duration of creation lasts for billions of years, and that the duration of destruction also lasts for billions of years, they are the knowers of the cycles of creation and destruction. (8.17)

avyaktād vyaktayaḥ sarvāḥ prabhavantyahar-āgame
rātryāgame pralīyante tatraivāvyakta-sanjñake (8.18)
bhūta-grāmaḥ sa evāyaṁ bhūtvā bhūtvā pralīyate
rātryāgame 'vaśhaḥ Parth prabhavatyahar-āgame (8.19)

All manifestations come out of the primary material nature during the creative cycle, and they merge into the primary material nature during the destructive cycle. The same multitude of beings comes into existence again and again at the arrival of the creative cycle and is annihilated, inevitably, at the arrival of the destructive cycle. (8.18-19)

vedeṣhu yajñeṣhu tapaḥsu chaiva dāneṣhu yat puṇya-phalaṁ pradiṣhṭam
atyeti tat sarvam idaṁ viditvā yogī paraṁ sthānam upaiti chādyam (8.28)

The one who knows all this knowledge goes beyond getting the benefits of the study of the Vedas, performance of sacrifices, austerities, and charities; and attains salvation. (8.28)

Krishna was explaining very patiently, but Arjun still had a number of questions bothering him.

"You say you are the eternal spirit. What does it mean?" he asked.

"The eternal spirit or eternal soul is like light. It is there around you but is formless. You can't touch it. When there is light, the world can be seen. When light is not there, you can't see anything. It's the same with the eternal soul, that is me. Nothing exists without the eternal soul, without me. Nothing happens without me. People who think they are the doer of their actions, are foolish."

"But if they are not the doer, who is?" Arjun's question was valid.

"People think they are seeing the world, but if there were no light, would they be able to see it? They forget they exist only because of me. They believe that they live their lives because of their own actions. That is ignorance."

Krishna then goes on to explain some significant concepts that need to be understood first, before understanding the eternal soul.

The spirit, soul or *atma* that is inside all living beings is called *brahm* in Sanskrit. It not only supports living beings but also supports the whole universe. This is the formless nature of God, the eternal being. *Brahm* is beginningless, endless and changeless. It is eternal. *Brahm* is not to be confused with Lord Brahma. *Parabrahm, Paramatma* is the Supreme Being, who is the origin of everything, including *brahm* (spirit or *atma*).

The various powers of *brahm* are called *deva* (or *devi*). People worship these powers as individual gods and goddesses to get their worldly desires fulfilled.

Living beings take birth, have a limited life span, and die or change form. They are known as *jiva*.

Karma means action and its consequences. It is our *karma* that makes us take birth again and again, and it is our *karma* that also dictates the kind of life we lead once we are born.

"Why are we born again and again? How does the soul know when and where to be born?" Arjun asked.

"Whatever you desire at the time of death, is what you get after death. The soul goes to what the mind has been thinking about in its last moments. If a person is thinking of worldly things, his soul will be reborn in the world. Mostly people remember whatever thought has dominated most of their life."

"When a person is dying, how can he make sure that his soul comes to you and goes nowhere else?" Arjun wanted to know.

"By making sure that he is thinking of me at the time of his death."

"How is it possible to think of you at the time of death? We don't know when we will die!"

"Simple enough! Remember me at all times," said Krishna, laughing.

"Nothing in universe escapes the cycle of life and death, including the earth and the entire universe. Beyond everything that takes birth, lives and dies, there is something that is never born and never dies, which is constant and unchanging. That is the eternal spirit, the eternal soul. That is me. And that is where the person who thinks of me in his last moments goes when he leaves his body. He is never reborn. He is free."

Krishna goes on to reveal how everything around us has a fixed lifespan. Brahma's one day and night put together is 8.64 billion years, and the entire universe dissolves at the end of Brahma's lifespan of 100 years, which works out to 311 trillion 40 billion years.

"If Brahma is the creator, why is he also subject to birth and death?"

"Because Brahma is also a soul, to whom the Supreme Being has given the responsibility of creation. And like all other souls, Brahma is also under the cycle of life and death. However, at the end of his lifespan, he is liberated and goes to the Supreme Being."

To illustrate the concept of transmigration of soul, there is a story in Bhagwat Puran of Bharat, the eldest son of King Rishabh Dev and Jayanti, Indra's daughter. King Rishabh enthroned Bharat as the king of earth before he died.

King Bharat ruled for many years. Once he felt his son was old enough to handle the responsibility, Bharat handed over his kingdom to him and took *sannyas* himself. He started living in Pulhashram on the banks of river Gandaki, passing his time in the worship of God. He came to be known as Rajarishi Bharat.

One morning, as he was meditating near the river, his attention was caught by a pregnant doe jumping into the river. She was running away from a lion, whose roar could also be heard echoing behind her. Unfortunately, the doe could not save herself but gave birth to a fawn in the flowing water before dying.

Rajarishi Bharat rescued the fawn and took it to his hut. He started raising it with great affection.

Collecting soft grass and feeding it, keeping it warm by hugging it and watching it play, gave Bharat a lot of pleasure. Day by day, as his fondness grew for the fawn, Bharat became irregular in his daily routine.

Ultimately, the fawn grew into a deer and following its natural instinct, left the hut to join its mates in the forest.

This made Bharat so sad that even when he was dying, he was only concerned about the fawn. As a result, he was born a deer in his next life. Nevertheless, because of his devotion to God as Rajarishi, even in a deer's body, Bharat spent his entire life near the ashram. This time when he died, he was born as a human again and became the great sage Jadabharat.

This story tells us that actually it is in our hands where we are born in our next life. So, if we want to go to God, we should form the habit of remembering God before taking our food, before going to bed, after getting up in the morning, and before starting any work or study.

It is not difficult to form this habit, as the famous poet-saint Kabir once said, "Remember God just as the village woman remembers the water pot on her head. She speaks with others and walks on the path, but her hand keeps holding onto the pot."

9

Krishna reveals the DIVINE MYSTERY

Krishna reveals his real nature, inspiring awe and reverence in Arjun. His unmanifested form pervades everything, but Krishna himself remains detached from all of it. Material nature, working under his direction, produces all moving and non-moving beings. Krishna loves everyone the same, but he takes personal interest in his devotees because such a person is closer to him. It is like one gets more heat if one sits close to the fire. There is no unforgivable sin or sinner. The fire of sincere repentance burns all sins.

Shrī Bhagavan uvācha
idaṁ tu te guhyatamaṁ pravakṣhyāmyanasūyave
jñānaṁ vijñāna-sahitaṁ yaj jñātvā mokṣhyase 'śhubhāt
(9.01)

Krishna said: I shall reveal to you, since you are uncritical of me, the most profound secret transcendental knowledge together with transcendental experience. Once you know this, you will be freed from the miseries of worldly existence. (9.01)

mayā tatam idaṁ sarvaṁ jagad avyakta-mūrtinā
mat-sthāni sarva-bhūtāni na chāhaṁ teṣhvavasthitaḥ (9.04)

This entire universe is an expansion of mine. All beings depend on me like a chain depends on gold, and the milk products depend on milk. I do not depend on or am affected by them, because I am the highest of all. (9.04)

na cha mat-sthāni bhūtāni paśhya me yogam aiśhwaram
bhūta-bhṛin na cha bhūta-stho mamātmā bhūta-bhāvanaḥ (9.05)

Look at the power of my divine mystery. In reality, I the sustainer and creator of all beings, do not depend on them, and they also do not depend on me. In fact, the gold chain is nothing but gold. In the same way, matter and energy are different as well as non-different. (9.05)

yathākāśha-sthito nityaṁ vāyuḥ sarvatra-go mahān
tathā sarvāṇi bhūtāni mat-sthānītyupadhāraya (9.06)

Perceive that all beings remain in me—without any contact or without producing any effect—as the mighty wind, moving everywhere, eternally remains in space. (9.06)

sarva-bhūtāni kaunteya prakṛitiṁ yānti māmikām
kalpa-kṣhaye punas tāni kalpādau visṛijāmyaham (9.07)

All beings merge into my primary material nature at the end of a time-cycle (Kalpa), and I create them again at the beginning of the next cycle. (9.07)

prakṛitiṁ svām avaṣhṭabhya visṛijāmi punaḥ punaḥ
bhūta-grāmam imaṁ kṛitsnam avaśhaṁ prakṛiter vaśhāt (9.08)

I create the entire multitude of beings again and again with the help of my material nature. These beings are under control of the three modes of nature. (9.08)

gatir bhartā prabhuḥ sākṣhī nivāsaḥ śharaṇaṁ suhṛit
prabhavaḥ pralayaḥ sthānaṁ nidhānaṁ bījam avyayam (9.18)

I am the goal, the supporter, the Lord, the witness, the abode, the refuge, the friend, the origin, the dissolution, the foundation, the treasure-house, and the immutable seed. (9.18)

ananyāśh chintayanto māṁ ye janāḥ paryupāsate
teṣhāṁ nityābhiyuktānāṁ yoga-kṣhemaṁ vahāmyaham (9.22)

I personally take care of both spiritual and material welfare of those ever-steadfast devotees who always remember and adore me with single-minded contemplation. (9.22)

ye 'pyanya-devatā-bhaktā yajante śhraddhayānvitāḥ
te 'pi mām eva kaunteya yajantyavidhi-pūrvakam (9.23)

Even those devotees who worship the deities with faith, they also worship me, but in a wrong way. (9.23)

patraṁ puṣhpaṁ phalaṁ toyaṁ yo me bhaktyā prayachchhati
tadahaṁ bhaktyupahṛitam aśhnāmi prayatātmanaḥ (9.26)

Whosoever offers me a leaf, a flower, a fruit, or water with devotion; I accept that offering. (9.26)

samo 'haṁ sarva-bhūteṣhu na me dveṣhyo 'sti na priyaḥ
ye bhajanti tu māṁ bhaktyā mayi te teṣhu chāpyaham (9.29)

The Super-soul is present equally in all beings. There is no one hateful or dear to me. But those who worship me with love and devotion are very close to me, and I am also very close to them. (9.29)

kṣhipraṁ bhavati dharmātmā śhaśhvach-chhāntiṁ nigachchhati
kaunteya pratijānīhi na me bhaktaḥ praṇaśhyati (9.31)

Such a person soon becomes righteous and attains everlasting peace. Be aware, that my devotee shall never perish or fall down. (9.31)

man-manā bhava mad-bhakto mad-yājī māṁ namaskuru
mām evaiṣhyasi yuktvaivam ātmānaṁ mat-parāyaṇaḥ (9.34)

Always think of me, be devoted to me, worship me, and bow down to me. Thus uniting yourself with me by setting me as the supreme goal and the sole refuge, you shall certainly come to me. (9.34)

Arjun, by now, was listening intently to Krishna, like a good student.

"My dear Arjun, I shall explain to you my true nature, my divine mystery, knowing which, you shall be relieved of the miseries of existence," Krishna declared.

"Everything you see and do not see in the universe, comes from me, lives in me, is supported by me, yet they are not me. I contain the universe, but the universe cannot contain me."

Krishna simplified it further by saying that just like wind has no existence independent from the sky, the soul too has no existence independent from God. The mighty winds move constantly yet remain in the sky. Likewise, the souls move through different bodies, yet always exist within God.

The gold ornaments in various shapes and forms look different from each other but are basically the same, that is gold. In the same way, the entire universe may look different but is created from one source, that is God.

"I am the very source of creation. Although I am everywhere, I am not a part of this cosmic manifestation. Just like space remains unchanged and unaffected by all the activity in it, so do I remain detached from all activities of the beings in me."

"Prakriti or nature gives birth to things moving and unmoving and it is according to its laws that everything that is born eventually dies. I am the master of Prakriti, I set it in motion, and I direct its activities. Prakriti cannot exist without me, but I can exist with or without Prakriti."

The entire process of creation, preservation and dissolution is called Maya. The cycle of creation and destruction keeps on going, like turning the gold ornaments into gold again and then using that gold to make new ornaments.

Krishna tells Arjun that most people do not believe in one formless God pervading everything. They treat other beings badly because they do not see God in them.

These people perform rituals and sacrifices, praying to the deities who have forms and names, hoping for a good life in heaven after their death. Their sacrifices are rewarded, and they enjoy the fruits of their good deeds in heaven. But, once their rewards get over, these people return to earth again, back into the cycle of life and death.

"I am the ritual, the sacrifice, the holy herbs, and the divine chant. I am the *ghee*, the fire and the offerings. I am the father of this universe, the mother, and the support. I am knowledge and the syllable Aum. I am also the Vedas. I am the creation and the annihilation, I am the witness too, I am the basis of everything."

People do not realize that they are worshipping one God through all the deities.

"Those who understand my true nature, who see me in everything and everything in me, who also understand that the different deities are different versions of me, and who think of me at all times, are dear to me."

Krishna is God, the eternal mother of the soul. Like a mother never deserts her child who is entirely dependent on her, Krishna also takes responsibility of the souls who surrender to him.

"Anyone, whether they are soldiers, merchants, farmers or scholars, whether they have read the holy scriptures or not, whether they are considered as saints or sinners, whether they offer me great riches or just a handful of water—I will take care of them. I will give them what they need and protect what they have."

Krishna clarifies that he is not concerned with the material value of the offering, he is only concerned with the love with which the offering is made.

"And this is the divine secret, Arjun, that no action is good or evil if it is done as an offering to me with complete devotion."

People associate devotion to God with going to temples. However, Krishna says that devotion should become a part of daily life.

How?

While performing any action, we should be conscious that we are working for the pleasure of God. This way, we would be free from the *karmic* binding of good or bad results. Otherwise, when we perform our actions with the intention of fulfilling our self-interest, we become responsible for any sins we commit knowingly or unknowingly and according to the law of *karma,* we have to reap their *karmic* consequences. By renouncing self-interest, we destroy all *karmic* consequences of work.

"Even if one commits the most terrible of actions, if he decides to engage in devotional service to me, he is to be considered saintly because he has made the right decision. He quickly becomes righteous and attains lasting peace. My devotee never perishes!"

Krishna concludes by entreating Arjun to become his devotee, "Fix your mind on me in whatever you do, be devoted to me, make me your goal and when your days are done, you will surely come to me, never to return."

Devotion to God is so powerful that it can reform and transform even the worst of criminals. There is a classic example of this in our scriptures, that of Valmiki, the author of Ramayana.

Valmiki was originally a dacoit called Ratnakar. Raised by a hunter, the only skill Ratnakar had was hunting. But as his family grew, hunting was not enough to feed them. Ratnakar resorted to robbing the travellers. Many times, he would kill them too.

One day, Ratnakar was looking to rob someone, when sage Narad passed by. Just as he attacked the sage, Narad asked him why he was doing so. Ratnakar said that this was how he looked after his family—by hunting and robbing.

Narad asked, "When you do all this, you are committing a sin, for which you will suffer. Will your family members agree to suffer your *karmic* punishment with you?"

"Of course, they will!" Ratnakar responded immediately.

"Not so quick, my friend! Go and ask them. Ask your family if they are willing to accept your *karmic* punishment as they accept the money you get for them after robbing people. I will wait here for you," Narad suggested.

Confident about his family's response, Ratnakar tied the sage to a tree and rushed home to ask them.

"I bring you money and food after robbing people. A sage told me that it is a sin to rob. Would you be willing to share my sins when I face my *karmic* punishment?"

To Ratnakar's disappointment, nobody was willing to share his sins. They told him that he was doing his duty of feeding them; how he got the money was his responsibility. They never asked him to rob!

Heartbroken Ratnakar went back to Narad. He felt sorry for his deeds and wanted to know how to atone for his sins.

Narad told him to repeat the words *Ra-Ma* (the name of God Rama) over and over again, but somehow Ratnakar was unable to do so. Finally, Narad told him to repeat *Ma-Ra* (*mara* means to kill).

Ratnakar found it easy enough to do so and sat there under a tree and started chanting immediately. He did not realize that by constant chanting of *Ma-Ra-Ma-Ra-Ma-Ra,* he actually ended up chanting *Ra-Ma-Ra-Ma.*

Many years later, Narad returned and saw that Ratnakar was sitting exactly where he had left him, and ants had made an anthill over him. Narad removed the anthill and told Ratnakar that his meditation was fruitful, and he was forgiven by God. Such was the power of meditating on the name of God.

Since he was covered with *valmika* (anthill), Ratnakar was called Valmiki from then on.

10

Krishna explains his MANIFESTATIONS

After explaining the importance of loving devotion to himself, Krishna further reveals to Arjun that he is the source of all that exists. Arjun is convinced. He finally understands Krishna to be the origin and the Lord of all, but wants to know the details. Krishna tells him more, describing the personalities, objects and activities that display his magnificence. Finally, he concludes that the magnitude of his glory cannot be described in words, as he upholds infinite universes within a fraction of his being.

Shrī Bhagavan uvācha
na me viduḥ sura-gaṇāḥ prabhavaṁ na maharṣhayaḥ
aham ādir hi devānāṁ maharṣhīṇāṁ cha sarvaśhaḥ (10.02)

Krishna said: Neither the celestial controllers, nor the great sages know my origin, because I am the origin of celestial controllers and great sages also. (10.02)

buddhir jñānam asammohaḥ kṣhamā satyaṁ damaḥ śhamaḥ
sukhaṁ duḥkhaṁ bhavo 'bhāvo bhayaṁ chābhayameva cha (10.04)
ahinsā samatā tuṣhṭis tapo dānaṁ yaśho 'yaśhaḥ
bhavanti bhāvā bhūtānāṁ matta eva pṛithag-vidhāḥ (10.05)

Discrimination, Self-knowledge, forgiveness, truthfulness, control over the mind and senses, tranquillity, fearlessness, non-violence, equanimity, contentment, austerity, charity, fame, ill-fame—these diverse qualities in human beings arise from me alone. (10.04-05)

teṣhāṁ satata-yuktānāṁ bhajatāṁ prīti-pūrvakam
dadāmi buddhi-yogaṁ taṁ yena mām upayānti te (10.10)

To those whose minds are always united with me in loving devotion, I give the divine knowledge by which they can attain me. (10.10)

teṣhām evānukampārtham aham ajñāna-jaṁ tamaḥ
nāśhayāmyātma-bhāva-stho jñāna-dīpena bhāsvatā (10.11)

I dwell within their inner psyche as consciousness, and destroy the darkness born of ignorance by shining the lamp of transcendental knowledge, as an act of compassion for them. (10.11)

Arjun uvācha
vaktum arhasyaśheṣheṇa divyā hyātma-vibhūtayaḥ
yābhir vibhūtibhir lokān imāṁs tvaṁ vyāpya tiṣhṭhasi (10.16)

kathaṁ vidyām ahaṁ yogins tvāṁ sadā parichintayan
keṣhu keṣhu cha bhāveṣhu chintyo 'si bhagavan mayā
(10.17)

Arjun said: Please describe to me your divine opulence, by which you pervade all the worlds and reside in them. How may I know you and think of you, and while meditating, in what forms can I think of you, O Krishna? (10.16-17)

Shrī Bhagavan uvācha
aham ātmā guḍākeśha sarva-bhūtāśhaya-sthitaḥ
aham ādiśh cha madhyaṁ cha bhūtānām anta eva cha
(10.20)

Krishna said: I am the Supreme Spirit (or Super-soul) seated in the heart of all living entities. I am also the creator, maintainer and destroyer, or the beginning, the middle and the end of all beings. (10.20)

mṛityuḥ sarva-haraśh chāham udbhavaśh cha bhaviṣhyatām
kīrtiḥ śhrīr vāk cha nārīṇāṁ smṛitir medhā dhṛitiḥ kṣhamā
(10.34)

I am the all-devouring death, and also the origin of future beings. I am the seven goddesses or guardian angels presiding over the seven qualities of fame, prosperity, speech, memory, intellect, resolve and forgiveness. (10.34)

yad yad vibhūtimat sattvaṁ śhrīmad ūrjitam eva vā
tat tad evāvagachchha tvaṁ mama tejo 'nśha-sambhavam
(10.41)

Whatever you see as beautiful, glorious, or powerful, know it to spring from just a spark of my splendour. (10.41)

atha vā bahunaitena kiṁ jñātena tavārjuna
viṣhṭabhyāham idaṁ kṛitsnam ekānśhena sthito jagat
(10.42)

What need is there for all this detailed knowledge, O Arjun? Simply know that by one fraction of my being, I pervade and support this entire creation. (10.42)

Krishna was delighted to see Arjun's keen interest in listening to him. So, he decided to talk about his phenomenal attributes and magnificence.

"You are my beloved friend, so I will reveal this very special knowledge to you. You shall soon know me as the source of all power and divinity, the soul of all," declared Krishna.

Krishna or the universal soul (God) is the origin of the cosmos with all its universes and beings. The two aspects of the universal energy, Purush the Spirit and Prakriti the Nature united to create all beings.

"I am present everywhere. Everything in this world moves and happens due to my will. All emotions like intellect, wisdom, forgiveness, truth, joy, sorrow, fear, self-control and charity, originate from me."

The diverse qualities of human beings, whether good or bad, also have their origin in the universal soul.

Krishna explained how devotion to God leads to destruction of ignorance and rise of understanding. This understanding is the light that dispels darkness and reveals the universal soul present in us. When we ask the right questions, follow the right actions, our inner lamp of wisdom lights up and we snap out of the delusions of the material world. And like everything else, this also happens by the grace of God that is within us and around us.

Arjun, who was awestruck by his friend's revelations said, "O Krishna, you are the prime deity, the unborn and all-pervading. I believe in you. And it is true that neither the gods nor the demons can describe your divine glory. Only you can describe your divinity."

"Forgive me as my mind still wanders through numerous confusions. But please do tell me in what forms should I see you? Please tell me once more in detail about your glory, for my mind is still not satisfied."

Krishna smiled at Arjun's earnestness.

"My friend, there is no limit to my magnitude. I reside in the hearts of all beings. I am the bright sun among all the celestial bodies. I am Indra, the king of gods among the gods. I am the life-force in all beings. I am Brihaspati among the priests. I am the ocean among the water bodies. I am Narad among the celestial sages. I am Varun among the water gods. I am the wind in nature. I am Vasuki among all the serpents. I am Ganga among the rivers. I am Rama among all the warriors."

"Always know my dear Arjun that I am the beginning, the middle and the end of all creation. I am the origin of all existence, and I am the all-devouring death, which is the origin of things to come. I am the endless time; I am the wisdom in all beings; and among the Pandavas I am you!" Krishna said with a twinkle in his eye.

The moment we are born, we start dying from that very moment. Death is devouring every living entity at every moment, and the last or final stroke is called death itself. But as we know, only the body dies, the soul is immortal. The soul takes birth in another body. So, in a way, the death of one living being causes birth of another. It is the universal soul or Krishna who is the cause of and presence in every living entity, he is the birth and death of all.

On a serious note, Krishna added, "Always remember that every glorious creature whether living or non-living is a part of my existence. Know me to be all pervasive and omnipresent holding the universe in my divine power."

Krishna also controls the seven qualities or attributes of nature, which are: fame or glory; success or prosperity; speech, an instrument to spread knowledge; memory to draw upon the vast storehouse of ancient knowledge; intellect, the power to discriminate and maintain harmony; resolve or steadfastness; and forgiveness, the harbinger of peace.

"All things exist due to my entering into them as Super-soul," saying this, Krishna paused for Arjun to take it all in.

Once the universes are created, the universal soul or Krishna is manifested as Super-soul in every entity. The Super-soul is present as a witness in us, watching the drama of life. The drama goes on till the body dies and the soul gets reborn in another body. Finally, everything dies, the universe is annihilated and gets dissolved back into its source, the universal soul or Krishna. Hence, Krishna is the beginning of the universe, the maintainer of the universal manifestations, and the end of all energy.

Arjun heard Krishna, mesmerized. He felt blessed to hear the glories of Krishna. He also felt very proud that he had such a magnificent friend and guide during his time of need, to show him the way.

"What more can I say to you, Kunti-putra, as the list goes on endlessly? But know this, that what I have revealed thus far is only a tiny glimpse of my infinite glory. Anything extraordinarily beautiful and glorious should be considered as a fragmental manifestation of my splendour. There is nothing more you need to know O Arjun, than that the entire universe is supported on an infinitesimal fraction of me," Krishna concluded.

The fact that people do not understand that the many aspects of God they see as deities are actually parts of one God, is beautifully explained in the ancient parable of blind men and an elephant.

In this popular story, a group of blind men came across an elephant one day. Unfortunately, they did not know anything about such a being or an animal.

They started touching it, because that was the only way a blind person could identify something.

The first person felt the elephant's trunk and said that the creature was a giant snake. The second one felt the animal's ear and declared that it was most likely a giant fan. The third one felt one of the legs of the elephant and said that the animal was like a pillar. The fourth one felt the side of the animal and said that the creature was like a smooth wall. The fifth one felt the tail and declared that the animal was like a rope. Finally, the sixth one felt the tusk and announced that the animal was hard and smooth like a spear.

The blind men were partially correct and partially wrong. The parable shows that we think our personal, limited experience to be the absolute truth. If we try to understand other people's experiences and see their truths, then it is possible for us to learn the actual, complete truth, the universal truth.

11

Krishna reveals his own COSMIC FORM

Arjun requests Krishna to show his *Vishwaroop* or the infinite cosmic form. Krishna gives Arjun divine vision by which to see his dazzlingly brilliant, unlimited universal form, which reveals within him everything that ever was, or is now, or will be in future. Krishna declares, that as *Kaal* or Time, he is the destroyer of the three worlds. He also discloses that except for the five Pandavas, all the soldiers on the battlefield will be killed. He advises Arjun to fight fearlessly and guarantees him victory.

Arjun uvacha
evam etad yathāttha tvam ātmānaṁ parameśhvara
draṣhṭum ichchhāmi te rūpam aiśhwaraṁ puruṣhottama
(11.03)

Arjun said: O Lord, you are what you declare yourself to be. Now I desire to see your divine cosmic form, O Supreme Being. (11.03)

Shri Bhagavan uvācha
paśhya me Parth rūpāṇi śhataśho 'tha sahasraśhaḥ
nānā-vidhāni divyāni nānā-varṇākṛitīni cha (11.05)
paśhyādityān vasūn rudrān aśhvinau marutas tathā
bahūny adṛiṣhṭa-pūrvāṇi paśhyāśhcharyāṇi bhārata (11.06)
ihaika-sthaṁ jagat kṛitsnaṁ paśhyādya sa-charācharam
mama dehe guḍākeśha yach chānyad draṣhṭum ichchhasi
(11.07)

Krishna said: Behold my hundreds and thousands of multifarious divine forms of different colours and shapes. Behold all the celestial beings, the entire creation, animate-inanimate, and whatever else you like to see, all at one place in my body. (11.05-07)

na tu māṁ śhakyase draṣhṭum anenaiva sva-chakṣhuṣhā
divyaṁ dadāmi te chakṣhuḥ paśhya me yogam aiśhwaram
(11.08)

But you cannot see me with your physical eyes; therefore, I will give you divine eyes to see my majestic power and glory. (11.08)

Arjun uvacha
ākhyāhi me ko bhavān ugra-rūpo namo 'stu te deva-vara
prasīda
vijñātum ichchhāmi bhavantam ādyaṁ na hi prajānāmi
tava pravṛittim (11.31)

Arjun said: Tell me, who are you in such a fierce form? I bow before you, O God of gods, be merciful! You who existed before all creation, I wish to understand you, because I do not know your mission. (11.31)

Shri Bhagavan uvācha
kālo 'smi loka-kṣhaya-kṛit pravṛiddho lokān samāhartum
iha pravṛittaḥ
ṛite 'pi tvāṁ na bhaviṣhyanti sarve ye 'vasthitāḥ
pratyanīkeṣhu yodhāḥ (11.32)

I am death, the mighty destroyer of the world. I have come here to destroy all these people. Even without your participation in the war, all the warriors standing arrayed in the opposing armies shall cease to exist. (11.32)

tasmāt tvam uttiṣhṭha yaśho labhasva jitvā śhatrūn
bhuṅkṣhva rājyaṁ samṛiddham
mayaivaite nihatāḥ pūrvam eva nimitta-mātraṁ bhava
savya-sāchin (11.33)

Therefore, you should get up and attain glory. Conquer your enemies and enjoy a prosperous kingdom. I have already destroyed all these warriors. You are only an instrument. (11.33)

mayā prasannena tavārjunedaṁ rūpaṁ paraṁ darśhitam
ātma-yogāt
tejo-mayaṁ viśhvam anantam ādyaṁ yan me tvad anyena
na dṛiṣhṭa-pūrvam (11.47)

Pleased with you I have shown you, through my own yogic powers, this particular supreme, shining, universal, infinite, and primal form of mine that has never been seen before by anyone other than you. (11.47)

bhaktyā tv ananyayā śhakya aham evaṁ-vidho 'rjuna
jñātuṁ drașhṭuṁ cha tattvena praveșhṭuṁ cha parantapa (11.54)

However, through single-minded devotion alone, I can be seen in this form, can be known in essence, and also can be reached. (11.54)

mat-karma-kṛin mat-paramo mad-bhaktaḥ saṅga-varjitaḥ
nirvairaḥ sarva-bhūteșhu yaḥ sa mām eti pāṇḍava (11.55)

The one who does all actions for me, and for whom I am the Supreme goal; who is my devotee, who has no attachment, and is free from enmity towards any being; attains me. (11.55)

The revelations of Krishna regarding his manifestations had amazed Arjun.

"Dear Krishna, all my doubts and confusions are cleared now. I understand that you alone are the prime mover of the universe. But I wish to see your eternal, imperishable cosmic form." Arjun bowed his head and requested.

Hearing this, Krishna smiled and said, "Your human eyes cannot see my universal form, O Arjun. For that, I will grant you divine vision."

And so, Arjun was bestowed divine vision. The next moment, Krishna came into his *Vishwaroop* form, which was an unlimited, blazing, effulgent, universal form.

Arjun saw the magnificent cosmic form of Krishna having innumerable faces, adorned with divine ornaments, holding celestial weapons, emitting dazzling light, that was brighter and more glorious than a thousand shining suns. And in that form were hundreds and thousands of creatures of different colours and shapes.

There were living beings and non-living objects, suns, moons and other celestial bodies of varying sizes, and many more seen-unseen objects in that universal form of Krishna. All around there was a strong, sweet fragrance of sandalwood. It was a fascinating sight indeed!

Arjun was stunned. With folded hands, he offered prayers.

The cosmic form of Krishna was so huge in size that it filled the space between the heaven and earth. Arjun saw the entire universe within Krishna! Brahma seated on the lotus and Shiva with his serpents were also there, as were all the other gods and goddesses in Krishna's cosmic form.

Among the varied things and beings Arjun saw in the universal form of Krishna, there was one that was particularly scary. It was that of an all-devouring giant.

Seeing all the gods and goddesses, including his own relatives and friends, entering his gaping mouth,

Arjun asked nervously, "Who are you and what is your mission? Why are all these people entering your mouth to be destroyed?"

"Arjun, understand that I am *Kaal* or Time, the destroyer of the world. I will destroy these people even without you. No one can escape death," Krishna responded.

So, even if Arjun did not want to fight, the war on the battlefield of Kurukshetra would still happen. And in that war, all the Kauravas were to die as were most of the Pandava family. Death was unavoidable. Whether or not Arjun fought, they would die anyway.

"Therefore Parth, rise and pick up your bow. Go and perform your duty. Fight for your kingdom. Your action will only determine the manner of the death of these warriors, nothing more, as they are already destroyed by me, their *Kaal*."

According to Krishna, it was better for Arjun to perform his duty as a warrior and fight. The warriors on the battlefield were destined to die, Arjun was only an instrument and not the cause of their death. The cause of their death was their own *karmic* baggage from the past and their actions in the present.

We all carry our individual baggage from our past lives and spend this life in completing the leftover incomplete tasks, fulfilling the leftover desires. As our past decided our present, our present decides our future. The entire universe runs on this formula. Each soul functions independently, though they may live together. Basically, we all are just instruments for the execution of God's cosmic plan.

Suddenly it dawned on Arjun that he had been treating Krishna as a dear friend all these years, without realizing his real nature. So, he begged for forgiveness.

"O merciful Krishna, please forgive my mistakes, which I must have committed in the last many years. I did not know your real nature. Now I have seen and understood your cosmic form, please return to your original form, the form I am familiar with."

Arjun was in awe of Krishna's real nature, but it created a distance between them. As close friends, Arjun and Krishna shared a special bond, which he wanted to return to. He wished to see the form that he had always loved.

Krishna first manifested his four-armed form of Vishnu and then resumed his original two-armed form that was so very beautiful and dear to Arjun.

He said to Arjun that before him, no one had ever seen God in this cosmic form. Not even the scholars who studied the scriptures, nor those who did severe penance or charity, get this opportunity. Only those with pure Arjun-like devotion in their hearts can see God, get to know him, and go to him on leaving the earth.

Krishna emphasized on five things necessary to reach him. The first is, to dedicate all our work to God, selflessly. The second is to make reaching God our only goal in life. The third is to serve God through serving people, seeing every living being as an image of God. The fourth is detachment from the material world. Finally, the fifth is, feeling no hatred towards anyone in the world.

One who possesses these five qualities is sure to attain God. This is the substance of the entire teaching of Gita.

12

Krishna explains BHAKTI YOGA

Krishna emphasizes that the path of devotion is the highest amongst all spiritual practices. He explains that it is difficult to meditate upon the unmanifest aspect of God, whereas worshipping him is much simpler. He tells Arjun that if he is unable to absorb his mind in God then he should devote all his work to God, or else work selflessly, renouncing the fruits of his action.

Arjun uvācha
evaṁ satata-yuktā ye bhaktās tvāṁ paryupāsate
ye chāpy akṣharam avyaktaṁ teṣhāṁ ke yoga-vittamāḥ
(12.01)

Arjun asked: Between those ever steadfast devotees who worship your personal form, and others who worship the impersonal formless Brahm, whom do you consider having the best knowledge of yoga? (12.01)

Shri Bhagavan uvācha
mayy āveśhya mano ye māṁ nitya-yuktā upāsate
śhraddhayā parayopetās te me yuktatamā matāḥ (12.02)

Krishna said: Those ever-steadfast devotees who worship with supreme faith by fixing their mind on my personal form of God, I consider them to be the best yogis. (12.02)

adveṣhṭā sarva-bhūtānāṁ maitraḥ karuṇa eva cha
nirmamo nirahankāraḥ sama-duḥkha-sukhaḥ kṣhamī (12.13)
santuṣhṭaḥ satataṁ yogī yatātmā dṛiḍha-niśhchayaḥ
mayy arpita-mano-buddhir yo mad-bhaktaḥ sa me priyaḥ (12.14)

One who does not hate any creature, is compassionate, is free from the notion of 'I' and 'mine', is even-minded in pain and pleasure, is ever content, who has subdued the mind, whose resolve is firm, whose mind and intellect are engaged in dwelling upon me, who is devoted to me—is dear to me. (12.13-14)

yasmān nodvijate loko lokān nodvijate cha yaḥ
harṣhāmarṣha-bhayodvegair mukto yaḥ sa cha me priyaḥ (12.15)

The one by whom others are not agitated and who is not agitated by others, who is free from joy, envy, fear, and anxiety, is also dear to me. (12.15)

anapekṣhaḥ śhuchir dakṣha udāsīno gata-vyathaḥ
sarvārambha-parityāgī yo mad-bhaktaḥ sa me priyaḥ
(12.16)

One who is desireless, pure, wise, impartial, and free from anxiety; who has renounced the doer-ship in all undertakings; such a devotee is dear to me. (12.16)

yo na hṛiṣhyati na dveṣhṭi na śhochati na kāṅkṣhati
śhubhāśhubha-parityāgī bhaktimān yaḥ sa me priyaḥ
(12.17)

One who neither rejoices nor grieves, neither likes nor dislikes, who has renounced both the good and the evil, and is full of devotion; is dear to me. (12.17)

samaḥ śhatrau cha mitre cha tathā mānāpamānayoḥ
śhītoṣhṇa-sukha-duḥkheṣhu samaḥ saṅga-vivarjitaḥ (12.18)
tulya-nindā-stutir maunī santuṣhṭo yena kenachit
aniketaḥ sthira-matir bhaktimān me priyo naraḥ (12.19)

The one who remains the same towards friend or foe, in honour or disgrace, in heat or cold, in pleasure or pain; who is free from attachment; who is indifferent to censure or praise; who is quiet, and content with whatever he has; unattached to a place, a country, or a house; is equanimous, and full of devotion; that person is dear to me. (12.18-19)

ye tu dharmyāmṛitam idaṁ yathoktaṁ paryupāsate
śhraddadhānā mat-paramā bhaktās te 'tīva me priyāḥ (12.20)

Those faithful devotees, who set me as their supreme goal and follow, or just sincerely try to develop the above-mentioned nectar of moral values, are very dear to me. (12.20)

Arjun was listening attentively to Krishna all this while. He had understood that Krishna was God, and was his ultimate goal in life. And to reach that goal, performing his duty selflessly as a warrior was the right path. But then, after seeing the cosmic form of Krishna, Arjun had another question. He wanted to know which form of God should be worshipped—the formless cosmic one, or the various other forms of Krishna.

"Of course, worshipping my cosmic form is the best," responded Krishna. "But then, worshipping God with a form is easier and better for most people. A true devotee has faith in everything—the formless God and God with a form such as Rama, Krishna, Hanuman, Shiva, Devi, and others."

"Till now I have explained about the path of knowledge and the path of action. There is yet another path through which you can attain me—the path of devotion," Krishna declared.

"The path of devotion! What should be the qualities of a true devotee then?" Arjun wanted to know.

And Krishna had a list!

"A devotee for whom no one is put into difficulty and who is not disturbed by anxiety, who is steady in happiness and distress, is very dear to me. One who neither grasps pleasure nor grief, who neither laments nor desires, is very dear to me."

"A true devotee is constantly engaged—sometimes chanting, sometimes reading books about God. Whatever he does, he does not let a single moment pass without devoting his activities to God."

"A true devotee is never envious of anyone. He is always kind to everyone, even to his enemy. He thinks that if a person is behaving as his enemy, it must be due to their past bad relationship, thus it is better to ignore than to fight. Whenever a devotee is in trouble, he thinks that it is God's mercy upon him that he is not getting all the punishment he deserves. He is tolerant, and he is satisfied with whatever comes his way, accepting it as the grace of God. A true devotee is neither happy nor distressed over material gain and loss. If he loses anything that is precious to him, he does not lament."

Essentially, a true devotee obeys the elders, helps others in need, does not hurt anybody, is friendly to all, asks for forgiveness if anyone is hurt by him, is calm in all situations, and is grateful to those who help him. God loves and helps those who act in this way.

There is a story in the Bhagwat Puran about a young boy named Prahlad, a true devotee of Vishnu.

Hiranyakashipu was the king of demons. Wanting to be all-powerful, he performed severe penance, which pleased Brahma. In those days, this was the method of attracting the attention of gods and then asking for boons.

Hiranyakashipu was blessed by Brahma with the boon that he could not be slain by man or beast, in the day or night, inside his palace or outside, in air or on ground. This great boon made the demon-king feel invincible and he started terrorizing everyone on earth, in heaven and in the netherworld. He declared that he should be worshipped like a god, and anyone not doing so would be punished.

Hiranyakashipu had a son Prahlad, who was an ardent devotee of Vishnu. He refused to follow his father's orders. One day, the angry king called his son to court and shouted, "I hear that you have been worshipping Vishnu instead of me!"

"Yes father, I have," the boy said softly.

"Promise me that you will not worship Vishnu at all and will worship me!" the king demanded.

"I cannot promise that," said his son honestly.

"Then you will have to die!" the king shouted in anger.

"Not unless it is the wish of Lord Vishnu," Prahlad answered with hands folded and head bowed.

Hiranyakashipu ordered his guards to kill Prahlad. They tried many ways to do that—poisoning him, attacking him with deadly weapons, trampling him under giant elephants, getting him bit by poisonous snakes, throwing him into a river to drown, making him sit on a burning pyre, and many more. Prahlad could not be killed.

Finally, in anger and frustration, the king asked his son, "Who is saving you?"

"Lord Vishnu," answered Prahlad, simply.

"Where is your Vishnu? Show me!" the king challenged.

"He is everywhere," was the son's simple answer.

"Everywhere!" the king laughed. "Even in this stone pillar?" he asked pointing at one of the grand pillars in the court.

"Yes, even in that pillar," the son answered confidently.

"Then let him come and fight with me!" Hiranyakashipu challenged, hitting the pillar hard.

The stone pillar broke.

And Vishnu emerged as Narasimha, the man-lion avatar from the pillar.

He picked up Hiranyakashipu, placed him on his thigh, and killed him with his sharp nails on the threshold of the palace at dusk, thus nullifying the king's conditions of immortality.

This is how Prahlad was blessed by God for his deep faith and devotion.

Stories like these show that God looks after his true devotees under all circumstances. And that having faith in God makes us fearless.

13

Krishna explains CREATION AND CREATOR

Krishna had thus far talked about Karm Yoga or the path of duty, and Bhakti Yoga or the path of loving devotion to God. Now he talks about the theory of creation. Krishna explains that our body is like a miniature universe and is made up of five basic elements, earth, water, fire, air and ether. And the entire universe, including our body, has only one creator, who himself becomes the creation, like cotton becoming thread and cloth. He says that our body is a field, our soul is the knower of that field, and God is the supreme knower of the fields of all living beings.

Arjun uvācha
prakṛitiṁ puruṣhaṁ chaiva kṣhetraṁ kṣhetra-jñam eva cha
etad veditum ichchhāmi jñānaṁ jñeyaṁ cha keśhava (not numbered)

Arjun said, "O Keshav, I wish to understand what are Prakriti and Purush, and what are kshetra and kshetrajna? I also wish to know what is true knowledge, and what is the goal of this knowledge?

Shri Bhagavan uvācha
idaṁ śharīraṁ kaunteya kṣhetram ity abhidhīyate
etad yo vetti taṁ prāhuḥ kṣhetra-jña iti tad-vidaḥ (13.02)

Krishna said: Know me to be the creator of all creation and the knower of the field in all fields. Understanding of both the field and the knower of the field is considered by me to be true knowledge. (13.02)

ṛiṣhibhir bahudhā gītaṁ chhandobhir vividhaiḥ pṛithak
brahma-sūtra-padaiśh chaiva hetumadbhir viniśhchitaiḥ
(13.05)

Great sages have sung the truth about the field and the knower of the field in manifold ways. It has been stated in various Vedic hymns, and especially revealed in the Brahma Sutra. (13.05)

mahā-bhūtāny ahankāro buddhir avyaktam eva cha
indriyāṇi daśhaikaṁ cha pañcha chendriya-gocharāḥ
(13.06)

The field of activities is composed of the five great elements, the ego, the intellect, the unmanifest primordial matter, the eleven senses (five knowledge senses, five working senses, and mind), and the five objects of the senses. (13.06)

ichchhā dveṣhaḥ sukhaṁ duḥkhaṁ saṅghātaśh chetanā dhṛitiḥ
etat kṣhetraṁ samāsena sa-vikāram udāhṛitam (13.07)

Desire and aversion, happiness and misery, the body, consciousness, and the will—all these comprise the field and its modifications. (13.07)

jñeyaṁ yat tat pravakṣhyāmi yaj jñātvāmṛitam aśhnute
anādi mat-paraṁ brahma na sat tan nāsad uchyate (13.13)

The Super-soul has its hands, feet, eyes, heads, mouths, and ears everywhere, because it is all-pervading and omnipresent. (13.13)

sarvataḥ pāṇi-pādaṁ tat sarvato 'kṣhi-śhiro-mukham
sarvataḥ śhrutimal loke sarvam āvṛitya tiṣhṭhati (13.14)

He is the perceiver of all sense objects without the physical sense organs; unattached and yet the supporter of all; devoid of the three modes of material nature, and yet the enjoyer of the modes of nature by becoming a living entity. (13.14)

sarvendriya-guṇābhāsaṁ sarvendriya-vivarjitam
asaktaṁ sarva-bhṛich chaiva nirguṇaṁ guṇa-bhoktṛi cha (13.15)

He is inside as well as outside all beings, moving and unmoving. He is incomprehensible because of his subtlety. And because of his omnipresence, He is very near, residing in one's inner psyche; as well as far away in the Supreme Abode. (13.15)

bahir antaśh cha bhūtānām acharaṁ charam eva cha
sūkṣhmatvāt tad avijñeyaṁ dūra-sthaṁ chāntike cha tat
(13.16)

He is undivided and yet appears to exist as if divided in beings. He is the object of knowledge, and though appears as the sustainer, he is also the creator and destroyer of all beings. (13.16)

avibhaktaṁ cha bhūteṣhu vibhaktam iva cha sthitam
bhūta-bhartṛi cha taj jñeyaṁ grasiṣhṇu prabhaviṣhṇu cha
(13.17)

The Supreme Being is the source of all light. He is beyond darkness of ignorance. He is the Self-knowledge, the object of Self-knowledge, and seated in the inner psyche as consciousness of all beings, he is to be realized by Self-knowledge. (13.17)

jyotiṣhām api taj jyotis tamasaḥ param uchyate
jñānaṁ jñeyaṁ jñāna-gamyaṁ hṛidi sarvasya viṣhṭhitam
(13.18)

He is the source of light in all luminaries and is entirely beyond the darkness of ignorance. He is knowledge, the object of knowledge, and the goal of knowledge. He dwells within the hearts of all living beings. (13.18)

kārya-kāraṇa-kartṛitve hetuḥ prakṛitir uchyate
puruṣhaḥ sukha-duḥkhānāṁ bhoktṛitve hetur uchyate
(13.21)

The Spiritual Being enjoys three modes of material nature by associating with them. Attachment to the three modes of nature due to ignorance caused by previous Karma is the cause of birth of living entity as good and evil beings. (13.21)

puruṣhaḥ prakṛiti-stho hi bhuṅkte prakṛiti-jān guṇān
kāraṇaṁ guṇa-saṅgo 'sya sad-asad-yoni-janmasu (13.22)

The Supreme Spirit or the Super-soul in the body is the witness, the guide, the supporter, the enjoyer, and the controller. (13.22)

samaṁ sarveṣhu bhūteṣhu tiṣhṭhantaṁ parameśhvaram
vinaśhyatsv avinaśhyantaṁ yaḥ paśhyati sa paśhyati (13.28)

When one beholds one and the same Lord existing equally in every being, one does not injure anybody, because one considers everything as one's own Self. And thereupon attains the Supreme Abode. (13.28)

yathā prakāśhayaty ekaḥ kṛitsnaṁ lokam imaṁ raviḥ
kṣhetraṁ kṣhetrī tathā kṛitsnaṁ prakāśhayati bhārata
(13.34)

They who perceive, with the eye of Self-knowledge, the difference between the body (Matter) and the knower of the body (Spirit) as well as know the technique of liberation of the living entity from the trap of divine illusory energy (Maya), attain the Supreme. (13.34)

kṣhetra-kṣhetrajñayor evam antaraṁ jñāna-chakṣhuṣhā
bhūta-prakṛiti-mokṣhaṁ cha ye vidur yānti te param
(13.35)

Those who perceive with the eyes of knowledge the difference between the body and the knower of the body, and the process of release from material nature, attain the Supreme destination. (13.35)

Arjun sat attentively at Krishna's feet. He had understood by now that the soul was a separate entity from the body, and that it doesn't get affected when anything happens to the body.

But where is this soul and how is it different from the body? And what are the body and soul made of?

Thus far, Krishna had explained Karma Yoga and Dhyan Yoga to Arjun. From here on he explains Gyan Yoga to him, starting by explaining the difference between body and soul.

"The body is the field of activities or *kshetra* and the soul is the knower of the field or *kshetra-jna.* And whatsoever form of life that exists, regardless of size, is a combination of body and soul."

"In every living being, there are two souls, the individual soul and the Super-soul. The individual soul is the knower of its own body, but the Super-soul is the knower of all the bodies of all the species of life."

Krishna explained that the whole world, including our body, is made of five basic elements: earth, water, fire, air and ether. We have eleven senses: five sense organs (nose, tongue, eye, skin and ear); five organs of action (mouth, hand, leg, anus and urethra); and a mind that makes us feel emotions of love, hate, pain, etc. We smell through our nose, taste through our tongue, see through the eyes, feel touch through skin, and hear through our ears. Our senses and sense organs help us learn and do things.

There are six changes that the body goes through, as seen by us—it is born, it grows, it stays, it produces by-products, then it begins to decay, and in the last stage it vanishes. It clearly shows that the body is a non-permanent material object.

The material nature is called *Maya* and being an energy of God, it is eternal like God, the Super-soul. The soul inside our body is also called *Prana*. It supplies power to the body to do all the work. When it leaves the body, we die.

Since the body is material by nature, it seeks to enjoy the material world through the senses. When the senses encounter the sense objects, the body and mind experience pleasure. The nature of the body field is like any field—as you sow so shall you reap. The feelings it feels are the result of the interactions of the senses with the material world. The soul has nothing to do with it. A wise person understands this.

"The Super-soul is one, but all individual souls are unique, because while travelling through the various cycles of life and death, they acquire different traits."

How?

"A soul accumulates the *karmas* for all the activities performed by the body, which causes its repeated birth in different bodies. Souls are also born into bodies according to conscious or unconscious desires of the person at the time of their death."

Krishna explains that since every human is different, their spiritual journey is also different. Some follow the path of meditation, some read scriptures, while there are some who work selflessly doing meaningful tasks—three different paths, but one common goal, which is to understand the Super-soul.

The Upanishads describe the soul and Super-soul as two birds seated in a nest, or the heart, of a tree or human body. The soul-bird has its back towards the super-soul-bird and is busy enjoying the fruits of the tree.

The fruits represent the result of the body's *karmas*. When the fruit is sweet, the soul-bird is happy; when it is bitter, then naturally the bird is sad. Though the super-soul-bird is a friend of soul-bird, it doesn't interfere in its personal matters, preferring to sit and watch instead.

The soul-bird has to simply turn around to face the super-soul-bird to end its miseries. This freedom or free-will is with the soul-bird—to decide to turn towards or away from the super-soul-bird, or God. So, whatever path we follow, the goal should be to face the Super-soul.

There's an interesting fable to show how we forget to use our free-will and get fooled by our material body.

Once a pregnant tigress was attacking a flock of sheep. Unfortunately, at that very moment, she gave birth to a cub and died. The sheep took the cub with them and looked after him. Now this cub had never seen any animal other than the sheep he grew up with, so he behaved like them. He ate grass like them and even bleated like them.

One day another tiger attacked this flock of sheep. As they were running away to save their lives, the tiger was shocked to see a young grass-eating tiger cub running with them. So, instead of grabbing sheep, the attacking tiger caught hold of the cub. He was further surprised to see the young cub bleating, looking scared. He dragged the cub to a river and made him see his reflection.

The tiger said to the cub, "Look at your face, it's like mine." Then he gave the cub some meat to eat. The scared cub stopped bleating and tried eating the meat.

The tiger waited patiently, watching the grass-eating cub transform into what he actually was, a carnivorous animal. He said, "You are the same as me. Come, let's go back to the forest."

This is how our soul gets affected by its environment, which is our body, and starts to identify with it. We need to understand that we are not the body, but the soul, and the soul is a part of the Super-soul. The understanding that we, as our soul, should not be fooled by our body, and that we should be following the Super-soul, is true knowledge, according to Krishna.

14

Krishna explains the THREE MODES OF NATURE

Krishna explains the nature of material energy, the source of body and mind. Nature exists in the three modes of goodness (*sattva*), passion (*rajas*) and ignorance (*tamas*). *Rajas* is the creative aspect of nature, *tamas* is destructive and *sattva* is in between. A combination of these three modes or *gunas* forms the basis of a person's character. *Sattva* frees from sinful reactions. *Rajas* fills with unlimited desires for material enjoyment. *Tamas* causes laziness and delusion. Krishna emphasizes again that the power of devotion has the ability to help a person overcome the influence of the three modes of nature.

Shri Bhagavan uvācha
paraṁ bhūyaḥ pravakṣhyāmi jñānānāṁ jñānam uttamam
yaj jñātvā munayaḥ sarve parāṁ siddhim ito gatāḥ (14.01)

Krishna said: I shall once again explain to you the supreme wisdom, the best of all knowledge; by knowing which, all the great saints attained the highest perfection. (14.01)

mama yonir mahad brahma tasmin garbhaṁ dadhāmy aham
sambhavaḥ sarva-bhūtānāṁ tato bhavati bhārata (14.03)
sarva-yoniṣhu kaunteya mūrtayaḥ sambhavanti yāḥ
tāsāṁ brahma mahad yonir ahaṁ bīja-pradaḥ pitā (14.04)

The total material substance, Prakriti, is the womb. I impregnate it with the individual souls, and thus all living beings are born. O son of Kunti, for all species of life that are produced, the material nature is the womb, and I am the seed-giving father. (14.03-04)

sattvaṁ rajas tama iti guṇāḥ prakṛiti-sambhavāḥ
nibadhnanti mahā-bāho dehe dehinam avyayam (14.05)

O mighty-armed Arjun, with the three gunas (modes) or ropes—goodness (sattva), passion (rajas) and ignorance (tamas)—material nature binds the eternal individual soul to the perishable body. (14.05)

tatra sattvaṁ nirmalatvāt prakāśhakam anāmayam
sukha-saṅgena badhnāti jñāna-saṅgena chānagha (14.06)

Amongst these, sattva guna, the mode of goodness, being purer than the others, is illuminating and full of well-being.

O sinless one, it binds the soul by creating attachment for a sense of happiness and knowledge. (14.06)

rajo rāgātmakaṁ viddhi tṛiṣhṇā-saṅga-samudbhavam
tan nibadhnāti kaunteya karma-saṅgena dehinam (14.07)

O Arjun, rajo guṇa is of the nature of passion. It arises from worldly desires and affections and binds the soul through attachment to fruitive actions. (14.07)

tamas tv ajñāna-jaṁ viddhi mohanaṁ sarva-dehinām
pramādālasya-nidrābhis tan nibadhnāti bhārata (14.08)

O Arjun, tamo guna, which is born of ignorance, is the cause of illusion for the embodied souls. It deludes all living beings through negligence, laziness, and sleep. (14.08)

sattvaṁ sukhe sañjayati rajaḥ karmaṇi bhārata
jñānam āvṛitya tu tamaḥ pramāde sañjayaty uta (14.09)

The mode of goodness attaches one to happiness of learning and knowing the Spirit, the mode of passion attaches to action, and the mode of ignorance attaches to negligence by covering the Self-knowledge. (14.09)

sarva-dvāreṣhu dehe 'smin prakāśha upajāyate
jñānaṁ yadā tadā vidyād vivṛiddhaṁ sattvam ity uta
(14.11)

When the light of Self-knowledge glitters all the senses in the body, then it should be known that goodness is predominant. (14.11)

lobhaḥ pravṛittir ārambhaḥ karmaṇām aśhamaḥ spṛihā
rajasy etāni jāyante vivṛiddhe bharatarṣhabha (14.12)

When passion is predominant; greed, undertaking of selfish works, restlessness and excitement arise. (14.12)

aprakāśho 'pravṛittiśh cha pramādo moha eva cha
tamasy etāni jāyante vivṛiddhe kuru-nandana (14.13)

When inertia is predominant; ignorance, inactivity, carelessness, and delusion arise. (14.13)

guṇān etān atītya trīn dehī deha-samudbhavān
janma-mṛityu-jarā-duḥkhair vimukto 'mṛitam aśhnute
(14.20)

When one rises above the three modes of material nature that originate in the body, one attains immortality or salvation, and is freed from the pains of birth, old age, and death. (14.20)

Arjun uvācha
kair liṅgais trīn guṇān etān atīto bhavati prabho
kim āchāraḥ kathaṁ chaitāns trīn guṇān ativartate (14.21)

Arjun said: What are the characteristics of those who have gone beyond the three gunas, O Lord? How do they act? How do they go beyond the bondage of the gunas? (14.21)

Shri Bhagavan uvācha
māṁ cha yo 'vyabhichāreṇa bhakti-yogena sevate
sa guṇān samatītyaitān brahma-bhūyāya kalpate (14.26)

Krishna said: The one who offers service to me with love and unswerving devotion, transcends the three modes of material nature and becomes fit for Nirvana, or salvation. (14.26)

brahmaṇo hi pratiṣhṭhāham amṛitasyāvyayasya cha
śhāśhvatasya cha dharmasya sukhasyaikāntikasya cha
(14.27)

I am the basis of the formless Brahm, the immortal and imperishable, of eternal dharma, and of unending divine bliss. (14.27)

"I shall enlighten you about the supreme wisdom, the best of all knowledge," declared Krishna.

He then went on to tell Arjun how he is the mother and the father of the universe.

"The total material substance, called Brahm, is the source of birth, and it is that Brahm that I saturate, making possible the births of all living beings, Arjun."

As father, Krishna places the Spirit or the seed of his intelligence, into material nature or Matter, which results in the birth of all beings in the universe. Material nature is also known as Mother Nature, because it gives birth to the entire creation. But since material nature is also an aspect of Krishna, it is Krishna who is the real mother as well.

"Material nature has three modes (*gunas*)—goodness (*sattva*), passion (*rajas*) and ignorance (*tamas*). All living beings pass through these three modes or states, to do any action. Under the influence of the mode of goodness, one does good and right actions; under the influence of the mode of passion, one becomes selfish; and under the influence of the mode of ignorance, one does bad things or becomes lazy. Sometimes one mode becomes more powerful than the other two. Soon the living being becomes habituated and begins to be controlled by these three *gunas*."

Goodness, passion and ignorance, the three modes or attributes of material nature are always present in all human beings. However, they are never constant. At any given point of time, only one out of the three dominates. Under the influence of these attributes, our mind expresses itself in a variety of ways at different moments of changing environment.

A person living in a serene place, close to nature, or even one who is sitting in a calm environment, engaged in studying, will have a *sattvic* mind. The same person's mind, going to the market, surrounded by sensory pleasures, will change from *sattvic* to *rajasic*. And if, by chance, he orders something to eat and finds a dead fly in it, his mind will instantly change from *rajasic* to *tamasic*.

When the soul identifies with the body, it gets trapped by the modes of nature. It feels the changes in the body as its own changes and participates in the joys and sorrows of the body. The soul forgets its own reality. This is called delusion.

"Do the three modes of nature act on our mind all at one time or each separately at different points of time?" Arjun wanted to know.

According to Krishna, these modes are acting on our mind all the time. But at any given point of time, human personality works under the influence of one predominant mode, while the other two are subdued, but never totally absent.

When the mode of goodness is prominent, passion and ignorance are defeated, and the mind is filled with feelings of happiness. When the mode of passion is prominent, goodness and ignorance are defeated, and the mind is filled with desires, actions and attachments. When the mode of ignorance is prominent, passion and goodness are defeated, and the mind becomes unaware of its nobler duties. The fight is always going on.

"When a person is able to transcend these three modes, he can become free from birth, death, old age and their stresses and can enjoy nectar even in this life," said Krishna.

At this Arjun asked thoughtfully, "O my dear friend, please tell me how a man should overcome and transcend these modes of nature."

Krishna smiled and answered, "If a person is under the influence of *tamas* or ignorance, then they should stop being lazy and start helping others, which will bring them to the mode of *sattva* or goodness. Likewise, if a person is under the influence of *rajas* or passion, they should stop being greedy and start helping others, to enter the *sattvic* mode. Once in sattvic mode, devotion to God helps to transcend the three modes completely."

"Laziness destroys a person. Passion ties him to the world. Goodness frees him from the grasp of passion and laziness, but it cannot give him spiritual knowledge. For that, devotion to God is the only way," he added.

"How does one recognize such a person who has transcended the three modes of nature?" Arjun had a valid question.

"He who is unaffected by changes in material reactions, who regards pleasure and pain alike, who looks upon a stone and a piece of gold with an equal eye, who is unchanged in honour and dishonour, who treats friend and foe alike—such a person is said to have transcended the modes of nature."

"Such people always engage in full devotional service, not failing in any circumstance—they at once transcend the modes of material nature. They come to the level of Brahm!" Krishna concluded.

There is a very popular story that illustrates the three *gunas* or attributes of Nature.

Once a man was attacked by three robbers, as he was passing through a forest.

After robbing him of his money, the first robber said, "What is the use of keeping this man alive?"

He was about to kill him, when the second robber said, "What is the use of killing him? We can tie him to a tree and leave."

The robbers tied the man to a tree and went away.

After a while, the third robber returned and untied the man. "Come, I will show you the way out," so saying the robber led the man to a path going out of the forest.

In this little story, the forest represents the material world, the three robbers are the three modes of nature, and the man is the soul. The first robber is *tamas* or ignorance, that wants to destroy the soul. The second one is *rajas* or passion, that wants to tie the soul down to the material world. The third one is *sattva* or goodness, that shows the right path to the soul.

The important thing to note here is that *sattva* is also a robber, which can only show the way but not actually take us to God. That we have to do ourselves.

15

Krishna explains the SUPREME PERSON

Krishna describes the nature of the material world to Arjun by comparing it with an upside-down Peepal tree, with its roots above and branches below. The roots are in the heaven, originating from the Super-soul, from where everything in the universe originates. The trunk and the branches are all the life forms existing in the world. The leaves of the tree are the wisdom of the Vedas. Krishna is the sap that nourishes the entire tree.

Shri Bhagavan uvācha
ūrdhva-mūlam adhaḥ-śhākham aśhvatthaṁ prāhur avyayam
chhandānsi yasya parṇāni yas taṁ veda sa veda-vit (15.01)

Krishna said: The universe may be compared to an eternal tree that has its origin (root) in the Supreme Being and its branches below in the cosmos. The Vedic hymns are the leaves of this tree. One who understands this tree is a knower of the Vedas. (15.01)

adhaśh chordhvaṁ prasṛitās tasya śhākhā guṇa-pravṛiddhā viṣhaya-pravālāḥ
adhaśh cha mūlāny anusantatāni karmānubandhīni manuṣhya-loke (15.02)

The shoots of this eternal tree spread all over the cosmos. The tree is nourished by the energy of material nature; sense pleasures are its sprouts; and its branches of desires hang downward in the human world causing Karmic bondage. (15.02)

nirmāna-mohā jita-saṅga-doṣhā adhyātma-nityā vinivṛitta-kāmāḥ
dvandvair vimuktāḥ sukha-duḥkha-sanjñair gachchhanty amūḍhāḥ padam avyayaṁ tat (15.05)

Those who are free from pride and delusion, who have conquered the evil of attachment, who are constantly dwelling in the Supreme Being, with all their lust completely stilled, who are free from dualities of pleasure and pain; such wise ones reach my Supreme Abode. (15.05)

mamaivānśho jīva-loke jīva-bhūtaḥ sanātanaḥ
manaḥ-ṣhaṣhṭhānīndriyāṇi prakṛiti-sthāni karṣhati (15.07)

The individual soul in the body of living beings is a fragmental part of the universal Spirit, or consciousness. Bound by the material nature, the embodied soul struggles with the six sensory faculties (including the mind) of perception. (15.07)

śharīraṁ yad avāpnoti yach chāpy utkrāmatīśhvaraḥ
gṛihītvaitāni sanyāti vāyur gandhān ivāśhayāt (15.08)

Just as the air carries away fragrance from the flower; similarly, the individual soul carries away the mind and senses from the old physical body it leaves during death, to the new physical body it acquires in reincarnation. (15.08)

śhrotraṁ chakṣhuḥ sparśhanaṁ cha rasanaṁ ghrāṇam eva cha
adhiṣhṭhāya manaśh chāyaṁ viṣhayān upasevate (15.09)
utkrāmantaṁ sthitaṁ vāpi bhuñjānaṁ vā guṇānvitam
vimūḍhā nānupaśhyanti paśhyanti jñāna-chakṣhuṣhaḥ (15.10)

The embodied soul enjoys sense pleasures using six sensory faculties of hearing, touch, sight, taste, smell, which are grouped around the mind. The ignorant cannot perceive the embodied soul departing from the body or staying in the body and enjoying sense pleasures by associating with the material body. But those who have the eye of Self-knowledge can see it. (15.09-10)

yad āditya-gataṁ tejo jagad bhāsayate 'khilam
yach chandramasi yach chāgnau tat tejo viddhi māmakam (15.12)

I am the brilliance of the sun that illuminates the entire universe. The radiance of the moon and the brightness of the fire also come from me. (15.12)

gām āviśhya cha bhūtāni dhārayāmy aham ojasā
puṣhṇāmi chauṣhadhīḥ sarvāḥ somo bhūtvā rasātmakaḥ (15.13)

Permeating the earth, I nourish all living beings with my energy. As the moon, I nourish all plants with the sap of life. (15.13)

ahaṁ vaiśhvānaro bhūtvā prāṇināṁ deham āśhritaḥ
prāṇāpāna-samāyuktaḥ pachāmy annaṁ chatur-vidham
(15.14)

It is I who takes the form of the fire of digestion in the stomachs of all living beings, and combine with the incoming and outgoing breaths, to digest and assimilate the four kinds of foods. (15.14)

dvāv imau puruṣhau loke kṣharaśh chākṣhara eva cha
kṣharaḥ sarvāṇi bhūtāni kūṭa-stho 'kṣhara uchyate (15.16)

There are two kinds of beings in the cosmos, the changeable (perishable) Temporal Beings, and the unchangeable (imperishable) Eternal Being (Spirit). All created beings are perishable (subject to change), but the Spirit does not change. (15.16)

iti guhyatamaṁ śhāstram idam uktaṁ mayānagha
etad buddhvā buddhimān syāt kṛita-kṛityaśh cha bhārata
(15.20)

I have shared this most secret principle of the Vedic scriptures with you, Bharat. By understanding this, a person becomes enlightened and fulfils all that is to be accomplished. (15.20)

Krishna compared the material world with an upside-down Peepal tree.

"The involvement of man with this material world is like the eternal cosmic tree. For the person who is engaged in materialistic activities, there is no end to this tree. He continues to wander from one branch to another. There is no possibility of liberation from the chain of births and deaths for anyone who is attached to the tree. The only way out is to cut down the tree with the weapon of detachment."

Krishna then goes on to describe the cosmic Peepal tree that has its roots above and branches below.

"The stem or the trunk of the tree is the individual soul. The roots arise from the Supreme Being or God as he is the source of all beings. The branches are desires from which sprout the shoots of action that give rise to desire once again, in an endless cycle. The fruits of desire are the colourful, fragrant flowers (and fruits) that grow and bloom for a short while, eventually withering away and dying. The leaves are the words of wisdom of the Vedas. The knower of this cosmic tree is also the knower of the Vedas."

"As the branches reach closer to earth, they plunge in and become roots, from which new trees arise. Gradually a forest develops around the cosmic tree, hiding it completely."

This analogy denotes our state in the material world. The tree constantly grows as that is its nature. The branches of desires continue to spread, some of them taking deep roots and resulting in producing more desires. Surrounded by an ever-growing jungle of desires, we lose sight of the main cosmic tree, the trunk of which is our own individual soul. The sap running through the tree, giving it life and consciousness, is Krishna, the Super-soul.

"And therefore, I say to you Kaunteya, cut down the forest of desires with the axe of detachment, so that your soul is able to see where it comes from. Always remember that the goal of your soul is to merge with its source, that eternal place from which no one ever returns—and that place is me."

"But Krishna, it is not easy to detach and surrender to you!" Arjun reacted.

At this, Krishna smiled indulgently at his friend. "When one is free from the delusion caused by pride, he can begin the process of surrender."

"A person is born on earth, lives for a brief time and then passes away. But, for whatever time he spends in the world, he foolishly believes that he is the Lord of the earth. The whole world lives under this impression. People think that the land, this earth, belongs to them. Only when a person is freed from such a false notion, that he really becomes free."

Krishna goes on to explain how as sunlight he is the producer of food through plants. As sap in the plants, he is also the distributor of food in the plant itself. And as the fire of digestion in our body, Krishna also becomes the consumer of food. Therefore, with his energy, Krishna makes the earth habitable, nourishes the vegetation and even lights up the digestive fire in us, helping us to digest and assimilate our food, which further helps us to grow and thrive.

Krishna lists out certain disciplines to Arjun, following which one could lead a life of fulfilment.

The first thing to do is to free oneself from pride. Pride leads to delusion. Filled with a false sense of importance, and arrogance, people ignore the greater values of life. The next is to drop attachments. Since detachment is not easy, it is better to turn the direction of attachment towards God.

"A person must cultivate knowledge of what is actually his own and what is not. And, when he understands things as they are, he becomes free from happiness and distress, pleasure and pain. He becomes full of knowledge. Then it is possible for him to surrender to me."

The most important, and the most difficult discipline is to still or quieten the mind. And to still the mind, the senses need to be controlled. A still mind is free from the dualities of material nature like pleasure and pain, happiness and sadness. In this state of calmness, a person is able to connect with his soul and surrender to God. The purpose of life is thus fulfilled.

"The soul is divine; then how does it savour the objects of the senses?" Arjun seemed a little confused.

"The mind and senses, on their own, are lifeless. But the consciousness or the life-force of the soul activates them. This helps them to experience pleasure and pain from their thoughts, situations, persons, and objects of the senses. The soul identifies the experiences of the mind and senses as its own."

"The problem is that the happiness experienced through the mind and the senses is material, hence short-lived. But the soul is divine, eternal. So, regardless of the amount, the soul can never be satisfied with such material pleasures. It keeps searching for the ultimate source of happiness. The soul remains restless, till it merges with its source."

"I am seated as Paramatma in everyone's heart. From me are all actions initiated and from me come remembrance, knowledge and forgetfulness," concluded Krishna.

There is interesting story in the Upanishads about how the celestial gods also need to be taught a lesson sometimes.

The *devas* (celestial gods) and *daityas* (demons) were always at war, to take control of heaven. Sometimes the *devas* won and at others the *daityas*. Once when the *devas* had won the war, they became very arrogant. Their king, Indra became proud of his own strength and believed himself to be invincible.

God decided to teach him a lesson. He manifested as a powerful *yaksha* and challenged Indra to fight. The winner would be declared the real king of gods.

Indra thought it to be a small matter and sent Agni, the fire-God to destroy the *yaksha*.

"I am the fire-God and can destroy the entire world in an instant! Come and fight with me... show me how powerful you are!"

"Try burning this piece of straw first," the *yaksha* said, placing a little straw in front of Agni.

Agni laughed and moved forward to burn it but couldn't! Instead, he felt cold and powerless.

Indra was shocked to hear this and sent Vayu, the wind-God to fight the *yaksha*. For one who could turn the entire world upside-down in one breath, a piece of straw was nothing. But unfortunately, Vayu also returned defeated.

Finally, Indra decided to confront the *yaksha* himself. To his surprise, he found Goddess Uma instead.

"Who is that *yaksha* who defeated Agni and Vayu? Where has he gone?" Indra demanded to know.

"Your pride has blinded you, Indra. The powerful *yaksha* is none other than your own father, your source of power. You are powerless without him."

Realizing his mistake, Indra asked for forgiveness.

Krishna thus imparted the most secret knowledge to Arjun and revealed the eternal truths, one by one.

Arjun like a true devotee absorbed Krishna's words of wisdom.

He finally understood that the creation is changeable and does not last forever. It has a limited life span. The soul does not change and is eternal. Krishna is the Paramatma, Super-soul or the Supreme Being. He is the source of everything in the universe. The divine bliss, that the restless soul is constantly searching for, can only be attained by surrendering to Krishna. Those who realize that the mind and the senses are the cause of bondage, and the only way to break free is to turn them towards God, are on the right path.

Tulsidas, the author of Ramcharitmanas, is an excellent example.

As a young man, Tulsi was madly in love with his wife. Once she went away for a few days to her parents' house, in the neighbouring village across the river. Soon enough, Tulsi started missing her and decided to go and meet her right away.

It was a dark and stormy night. No boatman was willing to take Tulsi across. So, he decided to swim. Soon he saw something floating nearby, thinking that it was a log, he clung to it and swam across. It was after midnight when Tulsi finally reached his wife's house. He was hesitant to wake up the entire household, so didn't want to knock or call out his wife's name. Her room was on the second floor. Looking around for a way to reach her, Tulsi saw a rope hanging from her window. He happily caught that and went up to her room.

Tulsi's wife was astonished to see him and asked how he managed to come so late at night, that too in such terrible weather! He pointed at the window. When they looked out, both were shocked. There was no rope, it was a snake! Even what Tulsi assumed to be a log, was in fact, a floating dead body. His desire to meet his wife was so intense that it had blinded his mind.

Tulsi's wife said to him, "You desire me, which is just a body made of flesh and blood. But if you could have such an intense desire for God, you would certainly attain him and be free from the cycle of life and death."

Her words had a life-changing effect on Tulsi. He left home. By detaching himself from all the material pleasures and engaging in devotion to God, he went on to become the great saint-poet, Tulsidas.

16

Krishna explains the DIVINE AND DEMONIC

According to Krishna, there are only two types of human beings—the wise or divine and the ignorant or demonic. Most people have both good (divine) and bad (demonic) qualities. Krishna explains that the divine nature develops by following the mode of goodness *(sattva)* and demonic nature develops by associating with the modes of passion *(rajas)* and ignorance *(tamas)*.

Shri Bhagavan uvācha
abhayaṁ sattva-sanśhuddhir jñāna-yoga-vyavasthitiḥ
dānaṁ damaśh cha yajñaśh cha svādhyāyas tapa ārjavam (16.01)
ahinsā satyam akrodhas tyāgaḥ śhāntir apaiśhunam
dayā bhūteṣhv aloluptvaṁ mārdavaṁ hrīr achāpalam (16.02)

tejaḥ kṣhamā dhṛitiḥ śhaucham adroho nāti-mānitā
bhavanti sampadaṁ daivīm abhijātasya bhārata (16.03)

Krishna said: Fearlessness, purity of inner psyche, perseverance in the yoga of Self-knowledge, charity, sense-restraint, sacrifice, study of the scriptures, austerity, honesty, non-violence, truthfulness, equanimity, compassion for all creatures, absence of malice and absence of pride—these are some of the qualities of those endowed with divine virtues. (16.01-03)

dambho darpo 'bhimānaśh cha krodhaḥ pāruṣhyam eva cha
ajñānaṁ chābhijātasya Parth sampadam āsurīm (16.04)

The signs of those who are born with demonic qualities are: hypocrisy, arrogance, pride, anger, harshness, and ignorance. (16.04)

daivī sampad vimokṣhāya nibandhāyāsurī matā
mā śhuchaḥ sampadaṁ daivīm abhijāto 'si pāṇḍava (16.05)

Divine qualities lead to salvation, the demonic qualities are said to be for bondage. Do not grieve O son of Pandu, for you are born with divine qualities. (16.05)

tri-vidhaṁ narakasyedaṁ dvāraṁ nāśhanam ātmanaḥ
kāmaḥ krodhas tathā lobhas tasmād etat trayaṁ tyajet (16.21)

Desire, anger and greed are the three gates of hell leading to the downfall (bondage) of the individual. Therefore, one must learn to give up these three. (16.21)

tasmāch chhāstraṁ pramāṇaṁ te kāryākārya-vyavasthitau
jñātvā śhāstra-vidhānoktaṁ karma kartum ihārhasi (16.24)

Let the scriptures be your authority in determining what should be done and what should not be done. You should perform your duty following the scriptural injunction. (16.24)

"Dear Arjun, so far, we have discussed about the soul, the body and the Super-soul. Now I shall tell you about the people in this world. There are two types of persons—divine and demonic," declared Krishna.

Arjun nodded in agreement. He had seen many demonic (bad) people amongst his cousins, the Kauravas. And of course, his teachers and grandsire Bhishma Pitamah were amongst the divine (good) ones.

"The qualities of a divine person are honesty, nonviolence, truthfulness, freedom from anger, kindness, gentleness, modesty, forgiveness and freedom from envy and greed."

Krishna described twenty-six virtues of divine or saintly nature. Fearlessness, according to him, was a state of freedom from fears for present and future. Attachment to anything causes the fear of losing it and such fears can only be destroyed by detachment.

Attachment to an object in the modes of passion and ignorance, also gives rise to impure thoughts, leading the person away from goodness. Success on the path of goodness comes by steadfastly pursuing the goal despite the temptations and diversions on the way. This also means that the senses need to be controlled.

Compassion towards all living beings is another important aspect of divinity. It makes the person tolerant and forgiving. Such people are gentle in disposition and peaceful at heart, they are devoid of vanity or greed and embody simple living and high thinking.

"Hypocrisy, arrogance, pride, anger, harshness and ignorance are demonic qualities that lead a person away from God."

Krishna described the six demonic qualities that should be shunned, or else they would drag the soul deeper into the hellish pits of passion and ignorance.

Ruled by passion and ignorance, the demonic person believes that the world runs on desires, fulfilment of which gives happiness. Such people are full of fear and anxiety—fear of inability to fulfil their desires and anxiety of losing whatever they have achieved. Having achieved something, they become full of arrogance and have no hesitation in eliminating whosoever they think to be their enemy. And on failing to achieve the object of their desire, they lose control of their mind and become full of anger.

"But what about those demonic people who also perform extravagant sacrifices to appease God and indulge in charity for the poor?" Arjun wanted to know, considering that Krishna had told him that a sinner can also reach God through sincere devotion.

"That is hypocrisy. A demonic person does extravagant sacrifices to glorify himself. He is pretending to appease God, while at heart he despises those who are not equal to him in stature. He is ignorant, for he doesn't know that despising any living being means despising me who is living in that being."

Then Krishna went on to say that the demonic qualities bind a person down to the cycle of life and death, while the divine qualities help him attain freedom from it. And ended by saying, "Do not worry, son of Pandu, for you are born with divine qualities."

The souls carry their nature from the lives they have lived in the past. Whatever good or bad deeds they keep doing and whatever thoughts they accumulate, are carried forward in their next lives as their divine or demonic tendencies. Most people have both good and bad qualities. Getting rid of bad qualities and cultivating good ones is necessary for spiritual progress.

Using will-power helps many to avoid indulging in bad habits or wrong behaviour. But for most, it's the fear of God that helps them avoid the traps leading to demonic behaviour.

"How can I know what to do and what not to do?" Arjun asked. A very valid question, since what may seem right behaviour to some, may be absolutely wrong in the eyes of others.

"Avoid desire, anger and greed, as they are the three gates leading to self-destruction. A person who has read the scriptures knows this."

Krishna had spoken about desire earlier too as the reason behind a person committing sin. Unfulfilled desire led to anger, a demonic quality. Greed is excessive desire.

"So, follow the advice of the scriptures to know what to do or not to do. The ancient wisdom of the holy books will guide you on the right path," concluded Krishna.

In the context of no one having only good qualities, there is an interesting anecdote in Mahabharata.

Draupadi was the wife of five Pandav brothers, is well known. But before that, in one of her past lives, she was the daughter of a sage. Though she was beautiful and virtuous, she was not married. She prayed to Shiva for a husband, but she wanted five qualities in him.

Pleased with her prayers, Shiva appeared before Draupadi to grant her wish. She asked for a husband who would be noble, strong, a good soldier, handsome, and wise. Shiva said that it was not possible for one man to have all the five qualities, so she will be married to five different men in her next life. These men were the Pandavas.

17

Krishna explains the THREEFOLD DIVISION OF FAITH

Krishna discusses the three modes of material nature in detail and how they affect human behaviour. According to the nature of a person's mind, his faith could either be *sattvic* or *rajasic* or *tamasic*. The quality of life he leads is also determined by his faith as well as his choice of food. The three types of food—*sattvic, rajasic* and *tamasic*—affect our well-being to a great extent. Our every action, whether sacrifice or charity, is affected by the three modes of nature.

Arjun uvācha
ye śhāstra-vidhim utsṛijya yajante śhraddhayānvitāḥ
teṣhāṁ niṣhṭhā tu kā Krishna sattvam āho rajas tamaḥ
(17.01)

Arjun said: What is the mode of devotion of those who perform spiritual practices with faith but without following the scriptural injunctions, O Krishna? Is it in the mode of goodness, or passion, or ignorance? (17.01)

Shri Bhagavan uvācha
sattvānurūpā sarvasya śhraddhā bhavati bhārata
śhraddhā-mayo 'yaṁ puruṣho yo yach-chhraddhaḥ sa eva saḥ (17.03)

Krishna said: The faith of any person is in accordance with his own natural disposition that is governed by Karmic impressions. A person is known by his faith. One can become whatever one wants to be, if one constantly contemplates on the object of desire with faith. (17.03)

āhāras tv api sarvasya tri-vidho bhavati priyaḥ
yajñas tapas tathā dānaṁ teṣhāṁ bhedam imaṁ śhṛiṇu (17.07)

The food preferred by all of us is also of three types. So are sacrifice, austerity, and charity. (17.07)

āyuḥ-sattva-balārogya-sukha-prīti-vivardhanāḥ
rasyāḥ snigdhāḥ sthirā hṛidyā āhārāḥ sāttvika-priyāḥ (17.08)

The foods that promote longevity, virtue, strength, health, happiness, and joy are juicy, smooth, substantial, and nutritious. Persons in the mode of goodness like such foods. (17.08)

kaṭv-amla-lavaṇāty-uṣhṇa- tīkṣhṇa-rūkṣha-vidāhinaḥ
āhārā rājasasyeṣhṭā duḥkha-śhokāmaya-pradāḥ (17.09)

Foods that are very bitter, sour, salty, hot, pungent, dry, and burning; and cause pain, grief, and disease; are liked by persons in the mode of passion. (17.09)

yāta-yāmaṁ gata-rasaṁ pūti paryuṣhitaṁ cha yat
uchchhiṣhṭam api chāmedhyaṁ bhojanaṁ tāmasa-priyam (17.10)

The foods liked by people in the mode of ignorance are stale, tasteless, putrid, rotten and impure. (17.10)

aphalākāṅkṣhibhir yajño vidhi-driṣhṭo ya ijyate
yaṣhṭavyam eveti manaḥ samādhāya sa sāttvikaḥ (17.11)

Selfless service encouraged by the scriptures, and performed without the desire for the fruit, with a firm belief and conviction that it is a duty, is in the mode of goodness. (17.11)

abhisandhāya tu phalaṁ dambhārtham api chaiva yat
ijyate bharata-śhreṣhṭha taṁ yajñaṁ viddhi rājasam (17.12)

Service that is performed only for show, and aiming for fruit, know that to be in the mode of passion. (17.12)

vidhi-hīnam asṛiṣhṭānnaṁ mantra-hīnam adakṣhiṇam
śhraddhā-virahitaṁ yajñaṁ tāmasaṁ parichakṣhate (17.13)

Service that is performed without following the scriptures, in which no food is distributed, which is devoid of mantra, faith, and gift, is said to be in the mode of ignorance. (17.13)

dātavyam iti yad dānaṁ dīyate 'nupakāriṇe
deśhe kāle cha pātre cha tad dānaṁ sāttvikaṁ smṛitam (17.20)

Charity that is given as a matter of duty, to a deserving candidate who does nothing in return, at the right place and time, is considered to be charity in the mode of goodness. (17.20)

yat tu pratyupakārārthaṁ phalam uddiśhya vā punaḥ
dīyate cha parikliṣhṭaṁ tad dānaṁ rājasaṁ smṛitam (17.21)

Charity that is given unwillingly, or to get something in return, or looking for some fruit, is said to be in the mode of passion. (17.21)

adeśha-kāle yad dānam apātrebhyaśh cha dīyate
asat-kṛitam avajñātaṁ tat tāmasam udāhṛitam (17.22)

Charity that is given at a wrong place and time, and to unworthy persons; or without paying respect to the receiver, or with ridicule, is said to be in the mode of ignorance. (17.22)

aśhraddhayā hutaṁ dattaṁ tapas taptaṁ kṛitaṁ cha yat
asad ity uchyate Parth na cha tat pretya no iha (17.28)

Whatever is done without faith, whether it is sacrifice, charity, austerity, or any other act, is useless. It has no value here or hereafter. (17.28)

Arjun had understood the difference between wisdom and ignorance, he now knew that divine qualities should be cultivated, and demonic tendencies should be destroyed.

Krishna had explained the importance of reading scriptures to follow the right path in life. The knowledge contained in the holy books helped a person to shed his ignorance and become wise. But then, what about those people who had no access to these books? Arjun wanted to know about the fate of such people.

"What is the nature of faith or devotion of those people who have no knowledge of the scriptures?" he asked.

Krishna's answer was simple. "Faith is an aspect of human nature. Everyone has it. Those who do not follow the scriptures, also have it. They may not follow the holy books, but they follow their own logic, their own perception, their own belief system. The faith of a person stems from his basic nature, whether *sattvic* or *rajasic* or *tamasic*."

A *sattvic* person worships gods seeking nothing but blessings. His worship is selfless as are his other actions in life. A *rajasic* person worships gods related to wealth and power. He offers gifts to gods in return for fulfilment of his material desires. A *tamasic* person worships the spirits of the dead. He can be seen worshipping trees and graves.

"As the faith differs according to the mode of nature of a person, so does his food preferences," he added.

A *sattvic* person prefers to eat *sattvic* food, consisting of sweet, fresh fruits and vegetables, whole grains and legumes, fresh dairy products, nuts, natural sweets like dates, honey and jaggery, and minimal amounts of fat. The foods are easy to digest and promote good health, vitality and longevity. They also make the mind calm, contented, cheerful and spiritually inclined.

Rajasic foods stimulate the life forces in our body, including our mind and senses. They are bitter, sour, salty, spicy, and pungent; exciting to the tongue but disagreeable to the system, causing mental agitation and stress. Non-vegetarian foods are *rajasic.* People with *rajasic* temperament enjoy this kind of food as it enhances their passions.

Tamasic foods are essentially unhygienic and stale. Improper preparation or preservation can turn *sattvic* or *rajasic* food into *tamasic.* A *tamasic* diet taken for long term has a malignant effect on the body and dulls the mind.

"A person's mode of nature not only governs his faith, but also his fate," Krishna stated.

A *sattvic* person's faith leads him towards the pursuit of knowledge. A *rajasic* person is directed towards the pursuit of action, while a *tamasic* person's faith leads him to ignorance and delusion.

Krishna concluded by saying, "In fact, a person's attitude towards anything and everything in life, reflects his mode of nature."

"Tell me dear Krishna, how do I control my mind and body," Arjun pleaded. The task suddenly seemed enormous and complicated to him.

Krishna then told Arjun about three kinds of austerities—of deed, word and thought. Austerity does not mean self-denial. It is an intelligent way of living, avoiding unnecessary wastage of energy. Based on with what attitude these austerities are performed, they give different results.

To bow in respect before the gods, our parents, teachers and wise people, is the right thing for us to do. It is considered as austerity of deed, as is eating the right foods, keeping ourselves and our surroundings clean.

Austerity of word means to only speak the truth but avoid speaking it if it is hurtful to others. It is important to understand in any situation, whether being truthful is important or being quiet. Talking too much should also be avoided.

Austerity of thought comprises a calm mind with good thoughts. Also, our mind should be in our control, instead of constantly jumping from one thought to another.

"So, if a person practices these three austerities, would he become *sattvic*?" Arjun wondered loudly.

"No. *Rajasic* and *tamasic* people also practice these three austerities. What sets them apart is their *reasons* for practicing them. When it is done for worldly rewards, whether to gain other people's respect and admiration, or to win power and wealth for oneself, it is in the mode of passion or *rajas*. When the threefold austerity includes bodily harm and self-torture, and that too with no clear thought about why it's being done, then it is considered *tamasic*."

"The threefold austerity is *sattvic* only when it is done with complete faith in its wisdom, with the sole aim of gaining a better understanding of oneself," Krishna clarified.

Charity means giving. As with any action, charity also is of three kinds, *sattvic*, *rajasic* and *tamasic*.

"A gift that is presented without any thought of receiving one in return, is a *sattvic* gesture. Charity that is practiced out of a sense of duty, to a deserving person, at the right time, with no strings attached is considered to be charity in the mode of goodness."

"Anything offered reluctantly is said to be *rajasic*. Charity that is given unwillingly, or with the hope of some kind of return, or some future reward, or as a repayment of past favours, is considered to be in the mode of passion. *Rajasic* charity may fool the giver and the receiver, but not God."

"Charity which humiliates the recipient, which is unsuitable, or is done with contempt, is *tamasic* in nature. *Tamasic* charity causes harm to both the receiver and the giver. One should not give money or gifts to evil people, as they would use it to do wrong things. Any charity, done in ignorance, would naturally be harmful to the giver, as he is the one helping the sinner to sin more."

Actions create consequences depending on the faith behind them. Faithless actions do not produce any results.

"Any acts of sacrifice, austerity or charity,

performed without following the guidelines given in the scriptures are futile, Parth," concluded Krishna.

There is an interesting story in Mahabharata about Sage Bharadwaj's son Yavakrida. All his friends had mastered the Vedas, but he had not. Yava felt that he was failing his duty as a son, by not studying the scriptures. After all, his father was a learned sage, and it was expected that the son would follow his father's footsteps.

Vedas are supposed to be studied under the right teachers, and it takes years to master them. Yava knew that but had no patience to spend that much time in studies. He decided to practice the toughest of penance to get Indra's blessings. He tortured his body so much that Indra came before him to ask why he was hurting himself.

"I wish to be a great scholar of the Vedas, hence I'm undergoing penance to get that knowledge directly. Bless me."

Indra smiled and said, "Son, you are on the wrong path. Go home and find a good teacher. The right path to Vedas is through study only."

Yava did not give up. He continued the self-torture and declared that he would cut off his limbs if he did not succeed in acquiring knowledge through penance.

One morning, as Yava went to bathe in the river, he saw an old man on the riverbank, scooping a handful of sand and throwing it in the river. As Yava watched, the old man continued to do that over and over again.

His curiosity aroused, Yava went up to the man and asked him what he was up to.

"I'm building a bridge across the river for people to cross easily," the old man said matter-of-factly.

Yava laughed. "You must be crazy to think that you can build a bridge across this mighty river with handfuls of sand!"

"No crazier than expecting to understand the

Vedas through penance instead of studying under a teacher," the old man retorted.

Yava realized that the old man was Indra and begged him to bless him with the power to learn. Indra blessed him. Yavakrida studied and became a great scholar of the Vedas.

Instead of getting distracted, we must follow the right path with steady faith, and it will certainly lead us to our goal.

18

Krishna reveals the ULTIMATE TRUTH

Krishna tells Arjun that there is no difference between a Karma Yogi and *sannyasi*. A Karma Yogi gives up selfish attachment to the fruits of his work, whereas a *sannyasi* does not work for any personal gain at all. He also explains how a person's nature determines his role in the society, and that doing the prescribed duty meant for that role is never affected by sinful reactions. By Krishna's grace, Arjun's confusion and doubts vanish, and he gets ready to fight the battle.

Arjun uvācha
sannyāsasya mahā-bāho tattvam ichchhāmi veditum
tyāgasya cha hṛiṣhīkeśha pṛithak keśhi-niṣhūdana (18.01)

Arjun said: I wish to understand the nature of sannyas (renunciation) and tyaag (sacrifice). I also wish to know the difference between the two. (18.01)

Shri Bhagavan uvācha
kāmyānāṁ karmaṇāṁ nyāsaṁ sannyāsaṁ kavayo viduḥ
sarva-karma-phala-tyāgaṁ prāhus tyāgaṁ vichakṣhaṇāḥ (18.02)

Krishna said: The sages define renunciation as abstaining from all work for personal profit. The wise define sacrifice as the sacrifice of, and the freedom from, the selfish attachment to the fruits of all work. (18.02)

niśhchayaṁ śhṛiṇu me tatra tyāge bharata-sattama
tyāgo hi puruṣha-vyāghra tri-vidhaḥ samprakīrtitaḥ (18.04)

Now hear my conclusion on the subject of renunciation, for renunciation is of three kinds. (18.04)

yajña-dāna-tapaḥ-karma na tyājyaṁ kāryam eva tat
yajño dānaṁ tapaśh chaiva pāvanāni manīṣhiṇām (18.05)

Acts of selfless service, charity, and austerity should not be abandoned, but should be performed, because selfless service, charity, and austerity are the purifiers of the wise. (18.05)

etāny api tu karmāṇi saṅgaṁ tyaktvā phalāni cha
kartavyānīti me Parth niśhchitaṁ matam uttamam (18.06)

Even these obligatory works should be performed without attachment to the fruits. This is my definite advice. (18.06)

niyatasya tu sannyāsaḥ karmaṇo nopapadyate
mohāt tasya parityāgas tāmasaḥ parikīrtitaḥ (18.07)

Giving up one's duty is not proper. The abandonment of obligatory work is due to delusion and is declared to be in the mode of ignorance. (18.07)

duḥkham ity eva yat karma kāya-kleśha-bhayāt tyajet
sa kṛitvā rājasaṁ tyāgaṁ naiva tyāga-phalaṁ labhet (18.08)

One who abandons duty merely because it is difficult, or because of fear of bodily trouble, does not get the benefits of sacrifice, at it is being done in the mode of passion. (18.08)

kāryam ity eva yat karma niyataṁ kriyate 'rjuna
saṅgaṁ tyaktvā phalaṁ chaiva sa tyāgaḥ sāttviko mataḥ (18.09)

Obligatory work performed as duty, renouncing selfish attachment to the fruit, is alone regarded to be sacrifice in the mode of goodness. (18.09)

pañchaitāni mahā-bāho kāraṇāni nibodha me
sānkhye kṛitānte proktāni siddhaye sarva-karmaṇām (18.13)
adhiṣhṭhānaṁ tathā kartā karaṇaṁ cha pṛithag-vidham
vividhāśh cha pṛithak cheṣhṭā daivaṁ chaivātra pañchamam (18.14)

Sankhya doctrine describes five factors for the accomplishment of all actions. They are: the physical body, the seat of Karma; the ego, the doer; the organs of perception and action, the instruments; various bio-impulses; and the fifth is the presiding deities of the organs. (18.13-14)

śharīra-vāṅ-manobhir yat karma prārabhate naraḥ
nyāyyaṁ vā viparītaṁ vā pañchaite tasya hetavaḥ (18.15)

Whatever action, whether right or wrong, one performs by thought, word, and deed; these are its five causes. (18.15)

jñānaṁ jñeyaṁ parijñātā tri-vidhā karma-chodanā
karaṇaṁ karma karteti tri-vidhaḥ karma-saṅgrahaḥ (18.18)

The knowledge, the known and the knower, are the threefold driving force to an action. The eleven organs, the act, and the agent or the modes of material nature are the three components of action. (18.18)

na tad asti pṛithivyāṁ vā divi deveṣhu vā punaḥ
sattvaṁ prakṛiti-jair muktaṁ yad ebhiḥ syāt tribhir guṇaiḥ (18.40)

There is no being, either on earth or among the celestial controllers in heaven, who can remain free from these three modes of material nature. (18.40)

brāhmaṇa-kṣhatriya-viśhāṁ śhūdrāṇāṁ cha parantapa
karmāṇi pravibhaktāni svabhāva-prabhavair guṇaiḥ (18.41)

The division of human labour is also based on the qualities inherent in peoples' nature or their make-up. (18.41)

śhamo damas tapaḥ śhauchaṁ kṣhāntir ārjavam eva cha
jñānaṁ vijñānam āstikyaṁ brahma-karma svabhāva-jam (18.42)

śhauryaṁ tejo dhṛitir dākṣhyaṁ yuddhe chāpy apalāyanam
dānam īśhvara-bhāvaśh cha kṣhātraṁ karma svabhāva-jam
(18.43)

Those who have serenity, self-control, purity, patience, honesty, transcendental knowledge and belief in God, are labelled as intellectuals or brahmins. Those having the qualities of heroism, vigour, firmness, dexterity, not fleeing from battle, charity and administrative skills, are called leaders, protectors or kshatriyas. (18.42-43)

kṛiṣhi-gau-rakṣhya-vāṇijyaṁ vaiśhya-karma svabhāva-jam
paricharyātmakaṁ karma śhūdrasyāpi svabhāva-jam
(18.44)

Those who are good in cultivation, cattle-breeding, business, trade, finance, and industry are known as businessmen or vaishyas. Those who are good in service to others, in all types of menial work, are known as workers or shudras. (18.44)

yataḥ pravṛittir bhūtānāṁ yena sarvam idaṁ tatam
sva-karmaṇā tam abhyarchya siddhiṁ vindati mānavaḥ
(18.46)

One attains perfection by worshipping the Supreme Being—from whom all beings originate, and by whom all this universe is pervaded—through performance of one's natural duty for him. (18.46)

īśhvaraḥ sarva-bhūtānāṁ hṛid-deśhe 'rjuna tiṣhṭhati
bhrāmayan sarva-bhūtāni yantrārūḍhāni māyayā (18.61)

The Supreme Lord, as the controller abiding in the inner psyche of all beings, causes them to work out their Karma like a puppet mounted on a machine. (18.61)

iti te jñānam ākhyātaṁ guhyād guhyataraṁ mayā
vimṛiśhyaitad aśheṣheṇa yathechchhasi tathā kuru (18.63)

Thus, I have explained to you this knowledge that is more secret than all secrets. Ponder over it deeply, and then do as you wish. (18.63)

sarva-dharmān parityajya mām ekaṁ śharaṇaṁ vraja
ahaṁ tvāṁ sarva-pāpebhyo mokṣhayiṣhyāmi mā śhuchaḥ (18.66)

Renounce all Dharma of body, mind and intellect, and just surrender completely to my will with firm faith and loving devotion. I shall liberate you from all sins, and the bonds of Karma. (18.66)

kachchid etach chhrutaṁ Parth tvayaikāgreṇa chetasā
kachchid ajñāna-sammohaḥ pranaṣhṭas te dhanañjaya (18.72)

O Arjun, have you heard me with a concentrated mind? Have your ignorance and delusion been destroyed? (18.72)

Arjun uvācha
naṣhṭo mohaḥ smṛitir labdhā tvat-prasādān mayāchyuta
sthito 'smi gata-sandehaḥ kariṣhye vachanaṁ tava (18.73)

Arjun said: O Krishna, by your grace, my illusion has been dispelled, and I am situated in knowledge. I am now free from doubts, and I shall act according to your instructions. (18.73)

yatra yogeśhvaraḥ kṛiṣhṇo yatra pārtho dhanur-dharaḥ
tatra śhrīr vijayo bhūtir dhruvā nītir matir mama (18.78)

Sanjay said: Wherever there will be Krishna, the Lord of Yoga, and Arjun, a true devotee, wielding the weapon of self-control, there will be everlasting prosperity, victory, welfare and morality. (18.78)

In the battlefield of Kurukshetra, everyone waited for the conversation between Arjun and Krishna to end and the battle to begin. It seemed the sun had stopped moving in the sky and was waiting too.

Arjun did not look miserable anymore. He was listening attentively to whatever Krishna was explaining.

"I wish to know the difference between *sannyas* (renunciation) and *tyaag* (sacrifice). Is giving up something the same as not being attached to it?" he asked.

Krishna replied, "Giving up action is *sannyas,* while giving up attachment to the reward of action is *tyaag.* A Karma Yogi gives up selfish attachment to the fruits of his work, while a *sannyasi* does not work for any personal gain."

Krishna elaborated that giving up of desire-motivated action is renunciation, whereas giving up of fruits of action is sacrifice. Since desire is always for the fruit of action, renunciation and sacrifice seem similar in that respect. But there is a slight difference. One is in the present frame, the other is in the future.

According to Krishna, work should be done after eliminating both the factors. In which case, work becomes desireless action.

"One should never renounce the prescribed acts of duty, sacrifice, and charity. One should undertake actions as a matter of duty without any attachment to their fruits. Duties should be performed well, for the benefit of the entire humanity."

Krishna explained that the prescribed acts of duty, sacrifice, and charity become good or *sattvic* only when they are done without the doer wanting anything in return. Giving up any action for fear of physical discomfort is *rajasic*. Abandoning one's duties is *tamasic*.

"Know this Arjun, the person who performs his duties because they ought to be done, giving up attachment to the rewards of his actions, is a *sattvic* person. He is neither attached to actions for pleasure, nor is he repulsed because they cause him discomfort. Such a person escapes the cycle of rebirth and becomes one with me."

"You are a brave warrior Arjun, you must realize your duty and act accordingly, you should respond to the call of time," added Krishna

According to Krishna, there are five aspects of action: the first is the physical body, the second is the life-force, the third are the sense organs and limbs, and the fourth is the mind. The fifth aspect is the self-created destiny of the person, which comprises of the effects of past actions.

These five aspects are the doers of all actions, right or wrong. All actions that we do, through thought, word or deed, cannot happen without our body as their happening place. Neither can we perform any actions without our limbs and our sense organs as the instruments of performance. Our mind has an important role to play too; it processes everything that the sense organs sense and then decides what action to take. With everything in place, we need the energy to act, which is provided by our life-force. Finally, the fate comes into the picture. It is our own past experience that pushes us in a certain direction, making us choose one action over another.

"What makes one act?" Arjun queried.

"There are three factors. First, there is the object, which is perceived by our sense organs and interpreted by our mind. This is called 'knowledge'. Second is our own understanding about the object, based on what we have heard, seen or experienced in the past, which makes us love it, hate it, or be indifferent to it. This is called 'known'. Third, depending on our own feelings towards the object, we either choose to pursue it, reject it, or do nothing. This is called 'knower'."

So, even with the five causes or doers of action, we still need this three-fold driving force of knowledge, known and knower, to make an action happen.

The three modes of nature are also reflected in knowledge and action. A *sattvic* person's understanding will be *sattvic* and so will be his action. Likewise, for a *rajasic* or a *tamasic* person.

"You see Arjun, how no one is free from the three binding ropes of *gunas* of his own nature! A person's nature influences his thoughts, understanding and actions. According to their nature, people are classified as *brahmins, kshatriyas, vaishyas* and *shudras*."

Those who are good in learning, teaching, preaching, and guiding people in spiritual matters are called *brahmins* or intellectuals. Those who are able to defend the country, establish law and order, prevent crime, and administer justice are called *kshatriyas*, the warriors. Those who are good in farming, cattle-raising, business, trade, finance, commerce and industry are known as *vaishyas* or merchants. Those who are good in service and labour work are known as *shudras* or workers.

Arjun knew this, and also knew that he was a *kshatriya*.

Arjun's next question was, "How can anybody living and working in society attain liberation?"

"Work becomes worship when done as a service to God and without selfish attachment to the results. If you work honestly for which you are suited, you attain God. So, my dear Arjun, you are a *kshatriya* by nature, a warrior. Surrender to your nature. You have spent your entire life preparing for war. How can you not do what you are meant to do?"

Krishna paused and continued, "Kaunteya, I have revealed a secret, sacred knowledge to you. Think about it carefully and then make your decision."

"And do not worry my dear friend, I am always with you, to help you clear any doubts."

Arjun stood speechless, feeling overwhelmed with so many emotions—gratitude, happiness, love, respect, humility—Krishna had imparted such powerful knowledge to him, and also trusted him to use it in the right way.

Then Krishna spoke again, "Arjun, have you heard me attentively? Have I cleared up your doubts and worries?"

Arjun fell at Krishna's feet, with eyes streaming with tears. "My dear friend, all my doubts are gone, and I am free from conflicting thoughts. I am now prepared to act according to your instructions."

Krishna called out, "Get hold of your bow and fight for the noble cause, Arjun. The battlefield beckons you!"

Hearing Krishna's mighty call, the greatest archer in the world, felt new energy rushing into him. He drew himself up, and looking around dispassionately, raised the divine Gandiva and pulled the bowstring. And the battlefield reverberated with its mighty TWANG!

Amidst the sound of the conches, the neighing of war-horses, the trumpeting of war elephants, and the war cries raised by the soldiers, Arjun stepped forward to fight in the name of justice. And so, began the battle of Mahabharata on the plains of Kurukshetra, the war of good and evil!

Mahabharata is full of little stories. There is one about finding God while doing one's duty, instead of running away to the forest looking for him.

Kaushika was a young man, who wanted to follow the path of sages and become enlightened. So, he left his parents and went to the nearby forest to meditate and live a life of austerity.

After some time, with single-minded devotion, Kaushika acquired some spiritual powers. One day, as he sat under a tree meditating, a crane flew by crying out loudly. Kaushika looked up in anger and stared at the bird. The crane burst into flames. The

holy man felt sorry at the death of the bird, but also felt proud of his powers.

Like any monk, Kaushika would also go begging for his daily alms to nearby villages. That day he went to a small house to beg. The woman of the house went in to get some food for him. Now it so happened, that her husband also came home and asked for food. The woman first attended to her husband and told Kaushika to wait for a few minutes.

After her husband had been fed, she came out with food, saying, "I am sorry to have kept you waiting. Forgive me."

But Kaushika, feeling insulted, stared at her with anger. The woman smiled and told him that she was not a crane to die at his angry stare.

The holy man was naturally taken aback! He wondered how she knew of the crane incident.

As though reading his mind, the woman told Kaushika that he was unaware of the power of performing one's duty and that learning the scriptures was useless if he did not understand their true meaning. What was the use of such learning, when it cannot protect him from anger, one of the gateways of hell!

The woman then directed him to go to Mithila and meet Dharmavyadha to learn the secrets of doing one's duty with devotion.

On reaching Mithila, Kaushika realized that Dharmavyadha was known to everyone and was considered to be the greatest teacher in the region.

But the holy man was in for a shock—Dharmavyadha was a butcher by profession!

The butcher got up from his seat and asked, "Welcome honoured sir. Did that gentle woman send you to me? I know why you have come. Let us go home."

Dharmavyadha took the holy man to his house.

Kaushika saw a happy family, with the butcher's children running up to greet him. He saw the love and respect with which the butcher attended to his parents. Kaushika learnt from Dharmavyadha the lesson of doing one's duty. Selling meat was the butcher's family trade, which he was following dutifully, as sincerely as he was looking after his family.

Instead of going back to the forest, Kaushika returned home and began to look after his parents, a duty he had abandoned.

One can reach spiritual perfection by selflessly performing one's duty in life. This is the true worship of God, according to Krishna.

The Bhagavad Gita concludes with Sanjay telling the blind Kaurava king Dhritarashtra, that whatever strength of the army may be, victory will always be on the side of God and his true devotee.

THE END

Acknowledgements

Writing this book has been both a challenge and an immensely rewarding experience. I could not have completed it without the steadfast support of my husband, Avdhesh. Thank you for your endless patience and for understanding my moments of "spacing out."

To my beloved daughters, Shruti and Smriti, your encouragement and constant belief in me have been a source of strength and inspiration, pushing me to follow my dreams.

I am deeply grateful to my parents for teaching me that life's purpose is to know and understand oneself—only then can one truly understand others. Ma, thank you for always being my greatest fan.

A heartfelt prayer of gratitude goes to my grandfather, who planted the seeds of the Bhagavad Gita in my mind by gifting me a miniature version during my pre-teen years. Although he is no longer here to witness it, his gift has grown, much like the proverbial acorn, into a large tree that bears books on the Gita.

I owe special thanks to my publisher Kapish Mehra for nurturing that growth. My first book with Rupa explored Krishna's management skills including those from the Gita. The second book focused on the Gita's everyday wisdom. And now, with this third book, I present the Gita in a form meant especially for young readers.

Rudra, your willingness to be my sounding board, always providing a patient ear to my ideas, has been invaluable. I can't thank you enough. You have been the best commissioning editor I've ever worked with.

This journey would not have been possible without the strong foundation laid by my teachers and the unwavering support of my mentors. I am also deeply grateful to my readers and publishers, who have become my extended family. It's their ongoing encouragement that pushes me to write, reflect, and continue writing.

www.ingramcontent.com/pod-product-compliance
Lightning Source LLC
Chambersburg PA
CBHW020800160426
43192CB00006B/389
* 9 7 8 9 3 6 1 5 6 6 0 6 6 *